Test Yourself

Principles of Economics: Microeconomics

Kenneth Parzych, Ph.D.
Eastern Connecticut State University
Willimantic, CT

Contributing Editors

Jack Inch, M.A.
Oakland Community College - Orchard Ridge Campus
Farmington Hills, MI

Koula Mantzouranis, M.S.
Department of Business Administration
Broward Community College
Pembroke Pines, FL

James E. Howard, Ph.D.
Stephen F. Austin State University
Department of Business
Nacogdoches, TX

NTC LearningWorks
a division of NTC Publishing Group
Lincolnwood, Illinois

Library of Congress Cataloging-in-Publication Data
is available from the Library of Congress.

A *Test Yourself Books, Inc.* Project

97-98

97-98

Published by NTC Publishing Group
© 1996 NTC Publishing Group, 4255 West Touhy Avenue
Lincolnwood (Chicago), Illinois 60646-1975 U.S.A.
All rights reserved. No part of this book may be reproduced, stored
in a retrieval system, or transmitted in any form or by any means,
electronic, mechanical, photocopying, recording, or otherwise, without
prior permission of NTC Publishing Group.
Manufactured in the United States of America.

6 7 8 9 ML 0 9 8 7 6 5 4 3 2 1

Contents

Preface

Economics is an exciting and relevant discipline that relates to the well-being of individuals, nations, and the global community. It relates to the need to economize, to establish appropriate and achievable priorities, and to allocate resources efficiently to ensure the least-cost production and distribution of finished products and services for consumption.

Within a market-oriented economic setting, the allocative and distributive functions are determined by demand and supply, which represent the interaction of consumers and businesses. This results in market-determined prices within both the resource and product markets that may additionally be affected by government policies.

Principles of Economics: Microeconomics examines disaggregated economic concepts such as the behavior of individual consumers and businesses within the market setting. It seeks to explain individual product and resource price determination, demand and supply conditions that respond to market prices, and the use of resources in production. Demand elasticity is examined and its application to the tax and regulatory policy issues is also covered. In addition, short- and long-run production processes are reviewed and the principles of least-cost production and profit maximization are introduced. Also, the different forms of market structures, the regulatory initiatives of government to preserve competitive markets, and the characteristics of a nation's balance-of-payments are reviewed.

This work is intended to clarify and strengthen one's understanding of the basic and important concepts and issues in principles of microeconomics. It seeks to provide a very substantial and meaningful self-evaluation and to informatively enhance one's conceptual application of microeconomic analysis to relevant contemporary issues. Hopefully, it will also further one's appreciation and continued interest in the study of economics.

I express my indebtedness to my students and colleagues who have contributed to this work's completion. Most importantly, I dedicate this book to my wife, Mary, and our children.

Kenneth Parzych, Ph.D.

How to Use this Book

This "Test Yourself" book is part of a unique series designed to help you improve your test scores on almost any type of examination you will face. Too often, you will study for a test—quiz, midterm, or final—and come away with a score that is lower than anticipated. Why? Because there is no way for you to really know how much you understand a topic until you've taken a test. The *purpose* of the test, after all, is to test your complete understanding of the material.

The "Test Yourself" series offers you a way to improve your scores and to actually test your knowledge at the time you use this book. Consider each chapter a diagnostic pretest in a specific topic. Answer the questions, check your answers, and then give yourself a grade. Then, and only then, will you know where your strengths and, more important, weaknesses are. Once these areas are identified, you can strategically focus your study on those topics that need additional work.

Each book in this series presents a specific subject in an organized manner, and although each "Test Yourself" chapter may not correspond to exactly the same chapter in your textbook, you should have little difficulty in locating the specific topic you are studying. Written by educators in the field, each book is designed to correspond as much as possible to the leading textbooks. This means that you can feel confident in using this book, that regardless of your textbook, professor, or school, you will be much better prepared for anything you will encounter on your test.

Each chapter has four parts:

Brief Yourself. All chapters contain a brief overview of the topic that is intended to give you a more thorough understanding of the material with which you need to be familiar. Sometimes this information is presented at the beginning of the chapter, and sometimes it flows throughout the chapter, to review your understanding of various *units* within the chapter.

Test Yourself. Each chapter covers a specific topic corresponding to one that you will find in your textbook. Answer the questions, either on a separate page or directly in the book, if there is room.

Check Yourself. Check your answers. Every question is fully answered and explained. These answers will be the key to your increased understanding. If you answered the question incorrectly, read the explanations to *learn* and *understand* the material. You will note that at the end of every answer you will be referred to a specific subtopic within that chapter, so you can focus your studying and prepare more efficiently.

Grade Yourself. At the end of each chapter is a self-diagnostic key. By indicating on this form the numbers of these questions you answered incorrectly, you will have a clear picture of your weak areas.

There are no secrets to test success. Only good preparation can guarantee higher grades. By utilizing this "Test Yourself" book, you will have a better chance of improving your scores and understanding the subject more fully.

Introduction to Microeconomics

Brief Yourself

Economics examines the use of resources among individuals and nations within the global community. More of most things is typically preferred to less, and individual people and nations must prioritize their consumption and production objectives. Material wants are unlimited, but resources— land, labor, capital, and entrepreneurial ability—are scarce and must be allocated to fulfill insatiable consumption wants.

Macroeconomics examines broad aggregate concepts such as a nation's economic performance or global trends among nations. In contrast, microeconomics is concerned with the individual consumer or business behavior and performance.

The essence of economics and the need for individuals or a nation to prioritize objectives is embodied in the production possibilities function. It measures the varied quantities of products that can be produced and the opportunity costs of having more of something at the sacrifice of something else.

Capital goods are used in the production of other goods and most directly influence a nation's rate of industrialization. In contrast, consumer goods are produced for immediate consumption and determine a nation's standard of living.

The interdependence of economic activity is illustrated in the circular flow process. The resources of consumers are used by businesses in the production process, and the resource payments represent the income to be spent for the consumption of goods and services.

Test Yourself

1. What is economics?

2. How does microeconomics differ from macroeconomics?

3. Are individual's income or a company's product price and unit production costs examples of microeconomic or macroeconomic issues?

4. What is the nature of positive economics?

5. What are normative economic issues?

6. How does the production possibilities curve exhibit the principle of opportunity costs?

7. What are the opportunity costs of maintaining a nation's military forces?

8. What are capital or producer goods?

9. Will a nation's standard of living be most immediately increased with the production of consumer goods or capital goods?

10. Categorize the following products as either capital or consumer goods:

    a. machine tools

    b. automobile

    c. loaf of bread

    d. soap and detergents

    e. farm tractor

11. Can the production of capital goods be a measure of a nation's future rate of industrialization?

12. Can technological advances be represented by a movement from one point to some other point on a production possibilities curve?

13. What are the universal economic questions that all nations must address?

14. How do the universal economic questions influence a nation's economic system?

15. Does the question of what is to be produced relate to the production priorities of the nation?

16. How does the question of how a product is to be produced relate to the resource allocation question?

17. How are resources allocated within different economic systems?

18. How is the question of, for whom it is to be produced, answered?

19. How are finished products distributed within different economic systems?

20. What is the general purpose of drawing a circular flow diagram?

21. What are the principal sectors of economic activity within the circular flow process?

22. Describe the flows of economic activity between consumers and the business community within the resource markets.

23. Describe the flows of economic activity between consumers and businesses within the product market.

24. Describe how the government fits into the circular flow.

25. How do foreign trade activities have an impact upon the circular flow?

✔ Check Yourself

1. Economics is the study of the allocation of scarce resources—land, labor, capital, entrepreneurial ability — to satisfy a finite amount of any society's unlimited material wants. (**Nature of economics**)

2. Microeconomics examines disaggregate concepts that relate to an individual consumer or business. In contrast, macroeconomics examines broad economic concepts that may relate to a nation or the global economy. (**Nature of economics**)

3. These are microeconomic concepts since they relate to the individual consumers and businesses rather than the nation's entire population or business community. (**Nature of economics**)

4. Positive economics emphasizes recorded, documented information and answers the question "what is?." The actual size of the nation's public debt or recorded GDP for any year is an example of a positive economic statement. (**Nature of economics**)

5. Normative economics emphasizes subjective value judgements. "The nation's public debt should be reduced to zero," and "government must strive to further deregulate the nation's economy" are examples of normative economic statements. (**Nature of economics**)

6. The allocation of scarce resources to be used in the production of limited goods is exhibited by the production possibilities curve. A movement from one point to any other point on the curve shows that more of something requires the sacrifice of something else. Having to sacrifice or give up something is an opportunity cost. (**Production possibilities**)

7. Because of its limited budget, a nation must set priorities. Expenditures for military needs result in less monies spent on other non-defense products, programs, and services. These are opportunity costs. (**Production possibilities**)

8. Capital goods are not produced for immediate or direct consumption. Rather, they are typically purchased by business people to be used to manufacture other products or render services for sale. They are assets to a business. (**Production possibilities**)

9. Consumer goods are produced for immediate and direct consumption. Therefore, they most readily satisfy the consumers' material needs and contribute to a nation's standard of living. (**Production possibilities**)

10. a. Machine tools are capital goods used by businesses to produce other products. (**Production possibilities**)

    b. An automobile may be either a capital or consumer good. A car that is used by a business to facilitate production or service is a capital good. In contrast, a car that is owned and operated by an individual for personal use is a consumer good. (**Production possibilities**)

    c. A loaf of bread is a consumer good that is purchased for personal nutritional needs. (**Production possibilities**)

    d. Soaps and detergents that are purchased by consumers for personal use are consumer goods. If purchased by businesses for industrial uses or as a resource input, they may be considered capital goods. (**Production possibilities**)

    e. A farm tractor that is used in the production of agricultural products is a capital good. (**Production possibilities**)

11. The production of capital goods most directly determines a nation's capital stock and therefore increases its future ability to produce goods and services. It is a measure of future industrial growth. (**Production possibilities**)

12. A movement from one point to some other point represents a different combination of products or quantities of products to be produced. Technological advances are exhibited by a structural outward shift of the production possibilities curve. (**Production possibilities**)

13. The universal economic questions that all nations must address are:

    What is to be produced?

    How is it to be produced?

    For whom is it to be produced? (**Universal economic questions**)

14. How a nation decides to respond to the universal economic questions will determine its type of economic system. A market-oriented, socialist, or command type of economic system uniquely addresses these questions. (**Universal economic questions**)

15. The question of what is to be produced is central to any economic system. It relates to the nation's economic priorities and direction. The relative production of consumer goods would suggest an emphasis upon immediately increasing the population's standard of living, while the production of capital goods would emphasize industrialization and lesser quick gains in the nation's standard of living. (**Universal economic questions**)

16. How it is to be produced relates to resource allocation in the production process. The right combination of resources must be used in production to obtain maximum cost efficiency. (**Universal economic questions**)

17. Market forces within resource markets allocate resources into production in a market-oriented economy. The market determines resource prices and the levels of resource employment within the production process. In contrast, various levels of government intervention direct the allocation of resources within a socialist or command economy. (**Universal economic questions**)

18. The question about the product distribution is answered by income distribution in the resource market. (**Universal economic questions**)

19. Within a market-oriented economy, finished products are distributed to those individuals who can and will pay the price. The product price is determined by market forces within the product markets. In contrast, political processes and public officials and agencies direct the distribution of finished products within a socialist or command economy. (**Universal economic questions**)

20. The circular flow mechanism illustrates the interdependence of all economic activity within a nation's economy. (**Circular flow**)

21. The four dominant sectors of economic activity consist of:

    a. consumers

    b. businesses

    c. government

    d. foreign trade activity (**Circular flow**)

22. There is a flow of resources consisting of labor, capital, and entrepreneurial skills from consumers to the businesses. As payment, there is a reciprocal flow of resource payments from the business to the consumer sector that consists of wages, salaries, interest dividends, etc. These flows are determined by the market forces within the resource markets. (**Circular flow**)

23. Businesses employ resources to produce finished products that flow to consumers. Equally, consumers use their resource payments as income to buy the finished products produced. These flows are determined by the market forces within the product markets. (**Circular flow**)

24. Government policies have a diverse and significant impact upon the circular flows. The two most immediate influences result from government spending and taxation policies. Government regulations also have an impact upon both the resource and product markets. (**Circular flow**)

25. The most immediate and direct impact of foreign trade activities relates to the nation's export and import trade. Certain government policies may alter the international merchandise and financial flows among nations. (**Circular flow**)

Grade Yourself

Circle the numbers of the questions you missed, then fill in the total incorrect for each topic. If you answered more than three questions incorrectly, you need to focus on that topic. (If a topic has less than three questions and you had at least one wrong, we suggest you study that topic also. Read your textbook, or a review book, or ask your teacher for help.)

Subject: Introduction to Microeconomics

Topic	Question Numbers	Number Incorrect
Nature of economics	1, 2, 3, 4, 5	
Production possibilities	6, 7, 8, 9, 10, 11, 12	
Universal economic questions	13, 14, 15, 16, 17, 18, 19	
Circular flow	20, 21, 22, 23, 24, 25	

Capitalism and the Market System

2

Brief Yourself

Capitalism is a unique economic system that was described in the early writings of Adam Smith. Its noted characteristics include: the private ownership of manmade and natural resources; the notion of an economic vote in which consumers ultimately determine what is to be produced; the profit motive, which provides the incentive for business people to assume the risk and initiative of producing products or rendering services for sale; the expectation that competition exists among firms and between individuals; and a laissez-faire philosophy that assumes government must minimizes its influence within the economy. Additionally, it is assumed that the business and consumers act only in their self-interest.

The allocation of resources to the production of various goods and the distribution of finished products and services among consumers are dependent upon market conditions within resource and product markets.

Demand and supply conditions within markets will result in the determination of equilibrium prices, which ensures that quantities demanded by consumers will be equal to the quantities supplied by businesses. Shifts in demand or supply in response to non-price changes will result in new equilibrium prices and corresponding quantities.

The specialized production of products within certain regions of a nation and among nations within the global community characterizes the industrialization process. Specialization is based upon the principle of comparative advantage and is the basis for trade both domestically and internationally.

This chapter on capitalism and the market system also appears in the "Test Yourself" book entitled *Principles of Economics: Macroeconomics*. Understanding the characteristics of the market system is critical to a review of the fundamentals of both microeconomic and macroeconomic analysis.

Test Yourself

1. Identify the principal characteristics of a capitalist economic system.

2. What does the tenet of private property imply?

3. What is the principle of laissez-faire?

4. Why is competition among firms important within a capitalist economy?

5. What determines the allocation of resources and distribution of finished products within a capitalist economy?

6. What are some noted benefits of specialization?

7. What is the definition of a comparative advantage?

8. If two nations specialized according to their comparative advantage, what would be the net gain from specialization?

9. International trade is facilitated by the establishment of exchange rates. What are they?

10. What is the market mechanism?

11. Explain the Law of Demand.

12. How does the Law of Demand relate to the principle of diminishing marginal utility?

13. What determinants influence an individual's demand for goods and services?

14. What is change (shift) in quantity demanded?

15. What is a change in demand?

16. What are the income and substitution effects that determine the demand curve?

17. What are product substitutes?

18. What are product complements?

19. Indicate whether the following changes represent a change in quantity demanded or a change in demand:

    a. The consumer's tastes and preferences changed.

    b. The consumer won the $1 million in the state lottery.

    c. The selling price of the product changed.

    d. The price of a substitute product changed.

20. What are superior or normal products?

21. What are inferior products?

22. Define the concept of market supply.

23. What are other determinants of market supply?

24. Explain the difference between a change in quantity supplied and a change in supply.

25. Indicate whether the following changes represent a change in quantity supplied or a change in supply:

    a. New technology has increased labor productivity.

    b. Because of high industry profits, there has been an entrance of new firms producing the product.

    c. The selling price of the product has increased.

    d. Inflation has resulted in significant increases in resource prices and costs of production to the firm.

26. What is an equilibrium price?

27. Illustrate and explain the example of a market surplus.

28. Describe the existence of a market shortage and the resulting effect upon market price.

29. What is meant by the rationing function of prices?

30. Discuss the impact of an increase in demand upon the market.

31. Discuss the impact of an increase in supply upon the market.

32. Given market supply, what are the effects of a decrease in demand?

33. Given market demand, what are the effects of a decrease in supply?

34. Indicate whether the following products would be inferior or superior for a typical consumer:

    a. expensive servings of beef

    b. $5,000 automobiles

    c. around-the-world cruises

    d. a shirt from an outlet store

35. Indicate whether, for the typical consumer, the following paired products are substitutes or complements:

    a. gas and motor oil

    b. hamburgers and hot dogs

    c. peanut butter and jelly

    d. chicken and steak

36. What is exchange rate depreciation?

37. What is the impact of dollar devaluation upon U.S. exports and imports?

38. What is exchange rate appreciation?

39. What is the impact of dollar appreciation upon U.S. exports and imports?

40. What exchange rate policy initiative should a nation introduce to eliminate a balance-of-payments deficit?

✔ Check Yourself

1. The noted characteristics of a capitalist economic system include:

   a. private property

   b. primary role of consumers in determining what is produced

   c. self-interest and profit as the primary motive for production

   d. the existence of competition among industry firms

   e. a laissez-faire governmental philosophy (**Characteristics of capitalism**)

2. The tenet of private property means that manmade and natural resources may be privately owned and used for the benefit of that owner. (**Characteristics of capitalism**)

3. A laissez-faire philosophy is a belief that the least amount of governmental activity within a nation's economy is best. Government should not assume an active, direct, or aggressive role in domestic or international economic affairs. (**Characteristics of capitalism**)

4. Competition must exist if the market is to function efficiently as an allocative and distributive mechanism. If there are many firms within an industry, no one firm or select few firms can manipulate or direct the market price setting process. It additionally suggests that there are no substantial barriers to production and new firms are able to enter the industry. (**Characteristics of capitalism**)

5. The market forces of demand and supply allocate resources within the resource markets and distribute finished products and services within the product markets. (**Characteristics of capitalism**)

6. Specialization increases the cost efficiency that results from the division of labor and results in increased levels of output and enhances distribution of finished products into consumption. (**Comparative advantage**)

7. A comparative advantage exists when a nation has the greatest absolute advantage or the least relative cost. This principle is illustrated in Table 2.1.

   In this example the U.S. has an absolute advantage in the production of both products since it produces more of A and B than the UK does. Its absolute advantage is greatest in the production of product A. Its comparative advantage is in the production of the product.

   In contrast, the UK has an absolute disadvantage in the production of both products, but it is least with regard to the production of product B. Thus, its comparative advantage is in the production of product B. (**Comparative advantage**)

8. The U.S. produces 20 units of product A when two-thirds of its resources are used in its production. With specialization and the use of its entire resource base, the U.S. would then produce 30 units of product A.

   The UK produces 30 units of product B when one-third of its resources are used in its production. With specialization and the use of its entire resource base, the UK would then produce 90 units of product B. (**Comparative advantage**)

9. An exchange rate is the price of one currency in terms of another. If one U.S. dollar is exchanged for two UK pounds, the exchange rate is one-half dollar per pound or two pounds per dollar. (**Comparative advantage**)

Before Specialization			
Product A	**(% resources used)**	**Product B**	**(% resources used)**
20	(67)	40	(67)
_10_	(33)	_30_	(33)
30		70	
After Specialization			
Product A		**Product B**	
30	(100)	0	(0)
_0_	(0)	_90_	(100)
30		90	

Net gain from specialization is 20 more units of product B produced for distribution into consumption.

Table 2.1

10. The market mechanism provides for the interaction of consumers (demand) and businesses (supply) with regard to specific products and services. In the resource market, businesses purchase resources from households. (**The market system**)

11. The Law of Demand specifies the willingness and ability of a consumer to purchase increased quantities of a product at lower prices and smaller quantities at higher prices. (**Market demand**)

12. Consumer behavior exhibits the principle of diminishing marginal utility in which additional units of consumption yield lesser and lesser levels of utility or pleasure. Thus a consumer will buy more units of a product at a lower price and smaller amounts at a higher price. This is why the demand curve slopes downward, reflecting an inverse relationship between price and quantity demanded. (**Market demand**)

13. Many non-price determinants influence demand. They include:

    a. a consumer's level of income

    b. tastes and preferences

    c. a consumer's overall level of wealth

    d. expectations with regard to the consumer's overall economic well-being

    e. the prices of other products

    f. the number of consumers in the market (**Market demand**)

14. A change in quantity demanded is illustrated in Fig. 2.1. It is represented as a movement from one point to some other point on a demand curve in response to a change in the selling price of the product. On the given demand curve D_0 the initial product price was OP_0 and quantities demanded were OQ_0. Price increased to OP_1, and quantities demanded were OQ_1. The movement from point B to point A on the

demand curve is a result of the increased price. This is an example of a change in quantity demanded. The non-price determinants of demand remain unchanged. (**Market demand**)

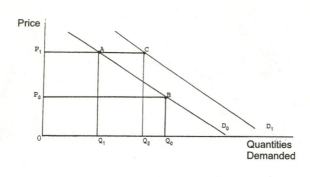

Fig. 2.1

15. A change in demand means that the selling price of the product remained constant and a non-price determinant changed. In Fig. 2.1, the initial selling price is OP_1 with corresponding quantity demanded of OQ_1. The movement from point A to point C and the increased consumption of the product from OQ_1 to OQ_2 at the same price results from a change in demand. More of the product is purchased at the same price, and it is represented by a rightward shift in the demand curve. A shift to the left indicates a decrease in demand. (**Market demand**)

16. The income effect relates to the effect of a price change upon a consumer's real income or actual disposable income. If the price of soda increases from fifty cents to one dollar per can, a consumer's real income declines. With one dollar of income, fewer cans of soda could be purchased.

    The substitution effect relates to the effect of a product price change upon the demand for other goods. At a higher price, a consumer may now substitute lower priced products for this product. (**Market demand**)

17. Products are substitutes if there exists a direct relationship between the change in price of one product and the resulting change in demand for the other product. If the price of product A increases (resulting in a decrease in quantity demand of product A), consumers will now buy more units of its substitute, product B, even though its price remained constant, representing an increase in the demand for product B. (**Market demand**)

18. Products are complements if there exists an inverse relationship between the change in price of one product and the resulting change in demand for the other product. If the price of product A increases (resulting in a decrease in quantities demanded of product A), consumers will now buy less of its complement, product B, even though its price remained constant. Consumers want more of one if they have more of the other and less of one if they have less of the other. (**Market demand**)

19. a. a change in demand

    b. a change in demand

    c. a change in quantity demanded

    d. a change in demand (**Market demand**)

20. A superior or normal product represents a direct relationship between a change in a consumer's income and the resulting change in consumption. The consumer buys more as income increases, and purchases less as income declines. (**Market demand**)

21. An inferior product has an inverse relationship between changes in a consumer's income and the resulting change in consumption. The consumer buys more as income declines, and purchases less as income increases. (**Market demand**)

22. A market supply function measures the relationship between product prices and the total quantities willingly supplied by producers. Quantity supplied is a function of product price, and a direct relationship exists. More is supplied as product price increases, and businesses will make less available for sale at lower prices. (**Market supply**)

23. In addition to product price, the other determinants of market supply include:

    a. resource prices

    b. the number of firms in the market

    c. the prices of other products

    d. innovations and technological changes

    e. government tax and subsidy policies (**Market supply**)

24. A change in quantity supplied results from a change in product price and is illustrated as a movement from one point to some other point on a supply curve. It assumes that the non-price determinants of supply have been constant.

    The move from point A to B in Fig. 2.2 is an example of a change in quantity supplied. As product price increased from P_0 to P_1, the quantities supplied increased from OQ_0 to OQ_1 representing movement along the supply curve S.

    In contrast, a change in supply is illustrated as the move from point B on S_0 to point C on S_1 and the corresponding increase in quantity from OQ_1 to OQ_2. Note that the selling price of the product remained constant but supply increased because of a change in a non-price determinant of supply. A change in supply is illustrated as a structural shift in the supply curve from S to S_1. More is supplied at the same price. A shift to the right represents an increase in supply, and a shift to the left represents a decrease. (**Market Supply**)

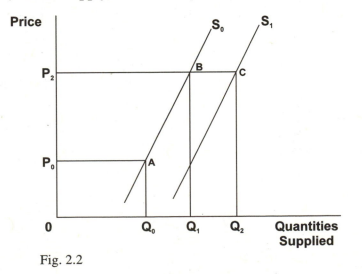

Fig. 2.2

25.   a. change in supply (increase)

    b. change in supply (increase)

    c. change in quantity supplied

    d. change in supply (decrease) (**Market supply**)

26. An equilibrium market price is determined by the interaction of demand and supply. It is the price at which the quantities demanded by consumers will be equal to the quantities supplied by businesses. The equilibrium price and corresponding equilibrium quantities are illustrated in Fig. 2.3 as P_e and Q_e. The market is cleared. (**Market analysis**)

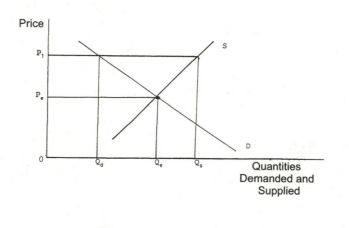

Fig. 2.3

27. A market surplus exists when quantities supplied exceed the quantities demanded. This is illustrated in Fig. 2.3 at a price of OP_1. Quantities supplied exceed quantities demanded and result in a market surplus of $Q_s - Q_d$. Prices will be bid down by suppliers and gravitate towards the equilibrium price. (**Market analysis**)

28. A market shortage exists when the price is lower than the equilibrium price, and quantities demanded exceed quantities supplied. This condition would exist in Fig. 2.3 for any price that is below the market equilibrium price of OP_e. A shortage of product results in prices being bid up as they gravitate toward the equilibrium price of OP_e. (**Market analysis**)

29. This implies that the competitive market forces of demand and supply will adjust toward unique determined equilibrium price where quantities demanded and supplied will be equal. (**Market analysis**)

30. The impact of a change in demand is illustrated in Fig. 2.4. The initial market equilibrium is at point A, with an equilibrium price of OP_0 and quantity of OQ_0. Demand increases to D_1 new market equilibrium at point B, with an equilibrium price of OP_1 and quantity of OQ_1. The increase in units produced is an example of an increase in quantities supplied or an upward movement along the supply curve from point A to point B. This resulted from the increase in product price, which occurred because of the upward shift or increase in demand. (**Market analysis**)

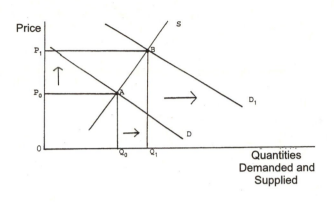

Fig. 2.4

31. The impact of a change in supply is illustrated in Fig. 2.5. The initial market equilibrium is at point A with an equilibrium price of OP_0 and quantities of OQ_0. Supply increases from S to S_1, and the new market equilibrium is point B with an equilibrium price of OP_1 and quantities of OQ_1. The increase in units consumed is an example of an increase in quantities demanded or a movement along the demand curve from point A to point B. This resulted from the lower product price that occurred because of the increase in supply. (**Market analysis**)

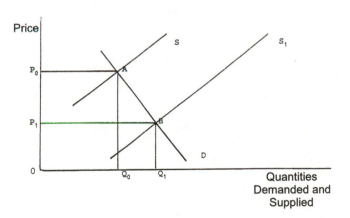

Fig. 2.5

32. A decrease in demand will result in a lower equilibrium price, along with a lower equilibrium quantity. It results in a decrease in quantities supplied or a downward movement along the supply curve, illustrated in Fig. 2.4 as a movement from point B to point A. (**Market analysis**)

33. A decrease in supply will increase the equilibrium price and decrease the equilibrium quantity. It results in a decrease in quantities demanded or an upward movement along the demand curve, illustrated in Fig. 2.5 as a movement from point P to point A. (**Market analysis**)

34. Tastes and preferences vary among consumers. However, for a typical consumer these items are likely to be:

    a. superior

    b. inferior

    c. superior

    d. inferior (**Market analysis**)

35. For a typical consumer, these items are likely to be:

    a. complements

    b. substitutes

    c. complements

    d. substitutes (**Market analysis**)

36. Exchange rate depreciation is a decrease in the price of one currency relative to another. If the U.S. dollar is devalued against the UK pound, the dollar is worth less in terms of pounds. In other words, each pound is worth a greater number of dollars. (**Exchange rate changes**)

37. The devaluation of the dollar means that U.S.–produced goods are less expensive for foreign consumers and foreign-produced goods more expensive for U.S. consumers. Thus U.S. imports should decrease and exports increase. (**Exchange rate changes**)

38. Exchange rate appreciation alters the convertible value of one currency to another. If the U.S. dollar were appreciated relative to the UK pound, it means that the dollar is worth more pounds. (**Exchange rate changes**)

39. The appreciation of the dollar means that U.S.–produced goods are more expensive for foreign consumers and foreign-produced goods less expensive for U.S. consumers. Thus, U.S. imports should increase and exports decrease. (**Exchange rate changes**)

40. A balance-of-payments deficit means that a nation's imports exceed its exports. To eliminate the deficit, a nation could devalue its currency to decrease its exports and lessen its imports. (**Exchange rate changes**)

Grade Yourself

Circle the numbers of the questions you missed, then fill in the total incorrect for each topic. If you answered more than three questions incorrectly, you need to focus on that topic. (If a topic has less than three questions and you had at least one wrong, we suggest you study that topic also. Read your textbook, or a review book, or ask your teacher for help.)

Subject: Capitalism and the Market System

Topic	Question Numbers	Number Incorrect
Characteristics of capitalism	1, 2, 3, 4, 5	
Comparative advantage	6, 7, 8, 9	
The market system	10	
Market demand	11, 12, 13, 14, 15, 16, 17, 18, 19, 20, 21	
Market supply	22, 23, 24, 25	
Market analysis	26, 27, 28, 29, 30, 31, 32, 33, 34, 35	
Exchange rate changes	36, 37, 38, 39, 40	

Demand and Supply Elasticity

3

Brief Yourself

Demand elasticity measures the responsiveness of consumers in adjusting their quantities demanded as a result of changes in product price along a given demand schedule. It quantifies how much quantity demanded will change in response to an initial change in price.

The demand schedule is elastic if consumers are very responsive to price changes and the resulting proportional change in quantity demanded is greater than the proportional change in price. The demand schedule is inelastic if consumers are not very responsive, so that the proportional change in quantity demanded is less than the proportional change in price. Unitary elasticity of demand implies that a given proportional change in price is matched by an equiproportional change in quantity demanded. Different levels of demand elasticity among consumers depend upon whether the products are necessities or luxuries, the availability of substitute products, the portion of a consumer's income that is spent on its purchase, and time.

Demand elasticity considerations are very important to the pricing decisions of businesses and public policy initiatives by government. There is a direct relationship between product price changes and total revenue collected by businesses when the demand for their product is inelastic. In contrast, price changes will be inversely related to total revenue when product or service demand is elastic. In seeking to maximize tax revenue collections, government typically imposes taxes upon those products and services for which demand is relatively inelastic.

Supply elasticity measures the producer response to proportional changes in product price in terms of proportional changes in quantity supplied along a given supply schedule. Market supply is elastic when the proportional change in quantity supplied is greater than the proportional change in price and inelastic if the proportional change in quantity supplied is less than the proportional change in price.

Cross elasticity of demand measures the responsiveness of demand for one product in response to a proportional change in the price of some other product. Products are substitutes if the cross elasticity coefficient is positive and complements if the coefficient is negative.

Lastly, income elasticity measures the relationship between income and the demand for different products. A direct relationship between proportional changes in income and demand implies a superior or normal product, and an inverse relationship suggests an inferior product.

Test Yourself

1. Define price elasticity of demand.

2. What is meant by an elastic demand for a product?

3. What is meant by an inelastic demand for a product?

4. What is meant by unitary elasticity of demand?

5. To interpret demand elasticity, it is recommended that the negative sign of the numerical coefficient be ignored and that the coefficient be expressed in absolute value. Why?

6. Explain the significance of an elasticity of demand coefficient that is greater than one, less than one, and equal to one.

7. Indicate the degree of elasticity for the following products when their calculated coefficients expressed in absolute values are:

   a. product a = 2

   b. product b = 1/2

   c. product c = 4

   d. product d = 1

   e. product E = 1/3

8. Explain how the elasticity coefficient is interpreted.

9. Determine the impact upon quantity demanded when:

   a. $E_d = 2$ and price increases by 3%

   b. $E_d = 1/3$ and price decreases by 6%

   c. $E_d = 1$ and price increases by 5%

10. Illustrate a demand curve that is perfectly elastic.

11. Illustrate a demand curve that is perfectly inelastic.

12. Explain and illustrate the varying degrees of demand elasticity along a linear demand curve.

13. Calculate demand elasticity at coordinate points A and B from the demand curve illustrated in question 12.

14. What factors determine the price elasticity of demand for a product?

15. Explain the importance of substitutes in determining the degree of demand elasticity.

16. Can advertising and brand-name promotions have an impact upon price elasticity of demand?

17. Explain the importance of relative expenditures for a given item in determining demand elasticity.

18. Is culture important in determining demand elasticity?

19. Explain the impact of product price changes upon a firm's total revenue when demand is elastic.

20. Explain the impact of product price changes upon a firm's total revenue when demand is inelastic.

21. What is the impact of a price change when the firm's product demand is unitary elastic?

22. The product price increased from $10 to $15 and quantity demanded declined from 100 to 80 units. Would the total revenue test suggest that the demand for the product is inelastic?

23. The product price decreased from $5 to $4 and quantity demanded increased from 10 to 20 units. Would this suggest that the demand for the product is elastic?

24. What product elasticity conditions will ensure government of the greatest amount of collected tax revenues?

25. Under what elasticity conditions will a firm be most able to pass an imposed tax on to consumers by increasing product price?

26. The demand for most food products is inelastic. As a result, what is the impact of overproduction upon market prices and farm incomes?

27. Define cross elasticity of demand.

28. What does a positive cross elasticity coefficient mean?

29. What does a negative cross elasticity coefficient mean?

30. What does the numerical coefficient of cross elasticity represent?

31. The cross elasticity between product C and product D is $E_c = -1/2$. What is the impact upon the demand for product D when the price of product C increases by 10%?

32. The cross elasticity between product H and product K is $E_c = +3$. What is the impact upon the demand for product K when the price of product H decreases by 2%?

33. Define income elasticity of demand.

34. What does a positive income elasticity coefficient mean? ($E_y = +$)

35. What does a negative income elasticity coefficient mean? ($E_y = -$)

36. What does the numerical value of the income elasticity coefficient represent?

37. The income elasticity for product R is $E_y = -2$. What would be the impact of a 3% decrease in income?

38. The income elasticity for product P is $E_y = +5$. What would be the impact of a 2% increase in income?

39. Define elasticity of supply.

40. What are some of the direct determinants of market supply elasticity conditions?

41. Is market supply more inelastic with a relatively short or long time period within which production can be changed?

42. Why does a longer time period suggest a more elastic market supply condition?

✓ Check Yourself

1. Price elasticity of demand measures the responsiveness of quantity demanded to changes in product price. It is measured as the percentage change in quantity demanded divided by the percentage change in price. (**Elasticity definition**)

2. The demand for a product is elastic if consumers are very responsive to changes in product price. Specifically, it means that the percentage change in quantity demanded is greater than the percentage change in product price. (**Elasticity definition**)

3. The demand for a product is inelastic if consumers are not very responsive to changes in product price. Specifically, it means that the percentage change in quantity demanded is less than the percentage change in product price. (**Elasticity definition**)

4. Unitary elasticity of demand exists when there is an equiproportional change in quantities demanded and product price. The percentage change in quantity demanded is equal to the percentage change in product price. (**Elasticity definition**)

5. The numerical value of a calculated elasticity coefficient will always be expressed as a negative value because of the inverse relationship between product price and quantity demanded, as represented by the Law of Demand. Thus, if the coefficient is –5, it should be expressed in absolute value as |5|. For interpretive purposes, this means that it is greater than one. If the coefficient were –1/2, it should be expressed in absolute value as |1/2|, which means that it is greater than zero but less than one. (**Elasticity definition**)

6. If the elasticity coefficient is greater than one, (E_d 1), it means that product demand is elastic.

    If the elasticity coefficient is less than one, (E_d), it means that product demand is inelastic.

    If the elasticity coefficient is equal to one, (E_d =1), it means that product demand is unitary. (**Elasticity definition**)

7. Price elastic demand for the following products is:

    a. elasticity of demand is elastic for product A

    b. elasticity of demand is inelastic for product B

    c. elasticity of demand is elastic for product C

    d. elasticity of demand is unitary for product D

    e. product E is inelastic (**Interpretation of elasticity**)

8. The elasticity coefficient measures the multiple by which quantity demanded inversely changes in response to a proportional change in product price. (**Interpretation of elasticity**)

9. (a) The price increase of 3% will decrease quantities demanded by a multiple of 2 or 6%.

    (b) The price decrease of 6% will increase quantities demanded by a multiple of 1/3 or 2%.

    (c) The price increase of 5% will decrease quantities demanded by a multiple of 1 or 5%. (**Interpretation of elasticity**)

10. The demand curve labeled D_e in Fig. 3.1 exhibits perfect elasticity. At the fixed price of OP, quantities demanded are indeterminate. Any increase in price will result in none of the products sold; and any decrease in price will not increase the amount of product sold. (**Interpretation of elasticity**)

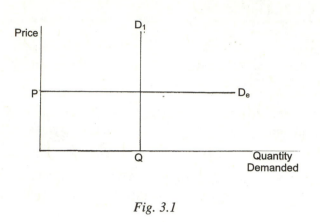

Fig. 3.1

11. The demand curve labeled D_i in Fig. 3.1 exhibits perfect inelasticity. At any price, the level of quantity demanded remains fixed at OQ. (**Interpretation of elasticity**)

12. The varying degrees of demand elasticity along a linear demand function are illustrated in Fig. 3.2. In general, demand is elastic within the range of prices above the midpoint M, inelastic within the range of prices below the midpoint M, and will approximate unitary conditions at the midpoint of the demand curve. (**Interpretation of elasticity**)

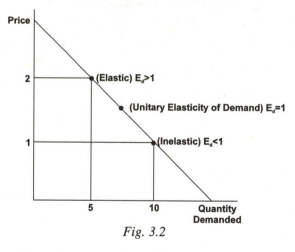

Fig. 3.2

13. Demand elasticity is calculated as the percentage change in quantity demanded divided by the percentage change in price.

   Thus, $$E_d = \Delta Q/Q \div \Delta P/P = (\Delta Q/\Delta P)(P/Q)$$

   When product price increases from 1 to 2, demand elasticity at coordinate point A is:
   $$E_d = \Delta Q/\Delta P(P/Q) = (-5/1)(2/5) = -10/5 = -2 = |2|$$

   Demand at the higher price of 2 is elastic.

   When product price decreases from 2 to 1, demand elasticity at coordinate point B is:
   $$E_d = \Delta Q/\Delta P(P/Q) = -5/1(1/10) = -5/10 = -1/2 = |1/2|$$

   Demand at the lower price of 1 is inelastic. (**Interpretation of elasticity**)

14. Some of the more direct determinants of demand elasticity include:

   (a) whether the product is considered a necessity or a luxury by the consumer

(b) the availability of substitutes

(c) the relative portion of a consumer's income that is spent to purchase the product

(d) the time over which a consumer responds to price changes (**Determinants of elasticity**)

15. The demand for a product is more elastic with greater amounts of available substitute products. Demand is less elastic or more inelastic with lessened numbers of product substitutes. (**Determinants of elasticity**)

16. Advertising can make the demand for a product more inelastic by reducing the level of acceptable product substitutability. Consumers identify with a product and will only buy the advertised trademarked items. (**Determinants of elasticity**)

17. Demand tends to be inelastic when the purchase of a product requires a small portion of the consumer's income. It tends to become elastic when the purchase represents a larger portion of income. Similarly, the relative importance of products varies with differences in income and wealth. A luxuriously priced yacht may be very necessary for a wealthy consumer while it would represent a very nonessential purchase for lower-income consumers. (**Determinants of elasticity**)

18. Consumer behavior is typically a conditional market response that is the result of many influences. Among them are the unique cultural and ancestral-conditioned influences upon individuals. These result in varying elasticity of consumer demands for ethnic foods, apparel, entertainment, and other manifestations of cultural behavior. (**Determinants of elasticity**)

19. There exists an inverse relationship between product price changes and the firm's total revenue when demand is elastic. An increase in product price results in a decrease in total revenue, and a decrease in price increases the firm's revenues. (**Applications of elasticity**)

20. There exists a direct relationship between changes in product price and the firm's total revenue when demand is inelastic. An increase in price will increase total revenue, and a price decrease will reduce the firm's total revenue. (**Applications of elasticity**)

21. Product price changes will not change a firm's total revenue when product demand is unitary elastic. A given proportional price change results in an equiproportional inverse change in quantity demanded, and total revenue will remain constant. (**Applications of elasticity**)

22. The firm's total revenue increased from $1,000 to $1,200 as price increased from 10 to 15. This confirms that the product demand is inelastic. (**Applications of elasticity**)

23. As product price declined, the firm's total revenue increased from $50 to $80. This confirms that demand is elastic. (**Applications of elasticity**)

24. Government will collect the greatest tax revenues when taxes are imposed upon products for which demand is inelastic. Since demand is inelastic, the imposed tax, increasing product price, will not significantly reduce quantity demanded. (**Applications of elasticity**)

25. The more inelastic product demand is, the greater the ability of businesses to pass the burden of additional taxes on to consumers by increasing price. (**Applications of elasticity**)

26. Overproduction will expand market supply and decrease food prices. Since the demand for food products is inelastic, the lower prices result in a decrease in revenues and incomes to farm producers. (**Applications of elasticity**)

27. Cross elasticity of demand measures the relationship between products. It calculates by what proportion the demand for one product will change in response to a proportional change in the price of another product. (**Cross elasticity of demand**)

28. A positive cross elasticity coefficient, (E_c 0), means that the two products are substitutes. Thus, there is a direct relationship between the direction of change in the price of one product and the resulting direction of change in demand for the other product. (**Cross elasticity of demand**)

29. A negative cross elasticity coefficient, (E_c −), means that the two products are complements. Thus, there is an inverse relationship between the direction of change in the price of one product and the resulting direction of change in demand for the other product. (**Cross elasticity of demand**)

30. The numerical coefficient for cross elasticity represents the proportional change in the demand for one of the products in response to a proportional change in price of the other product. If the cross elasticity between products A and B is $E_c = +2$, that means that they are substitutes, and the demand for one product will change directly by a multiple of twice the proportional change in price of the other product. (**Cross elasticity of demand**)

31. The cross elasticity of -1/2 confirms that the products are complements and that the demand for product D will change by a multiple of one-half the proportional change in the price of product C. Thus, an increase in the price of product C by 10% will decrease the demand for product D by 5%. (**Cross elasticity of demand**)

32. The cross elasticity of +3 confirms that the products are substitutes and that the demand for product K will change by a multiple of three times the proportional change in the price of product H. Thus, a 2% decrease in the price of product H will decrease the demand for product K by 6%. (**Cross elasticity of demand**)

33. Income elasticity of demand measures the responsiveness of demand to proportional changes in income. It is calculated as the percentage change in demand divided by the percentage change in income. (**Income elasticity of demand**)

34. A positive income elasticity coefficient confirms a direct relationship between changes in income and changes in the demand for the product. This indicates a superior (or normal) product. (**Income elasticity of demand**)

35. A negative income elasticity coefficient confirms an inverse relationship between proportional changes in income and proportional changes in the demand for the product. This indicates an inferior product. (**Income elasticity of demand**)

36. The numerical value of the income elasticity coefficient measures the multiple change in the demand for the product in response to a proportional change in income. If the income elasticity coefficient were $E_y = +2$ and income were forecasted to increase by 5%, the would mean that the demand for the product would increase by a multiple of 2 or 10%. (**Income elasticity of demand**)

37. Product R is an inferior product. Thus, a forecasted decrease in income of 3% will increase the demand for product R by 6%. (**Income elasticity of demand**)

38. Product P is a superior product. Thus, a forecasted increase in income of 2% will increase the demand for product P by 10%. (**Income elasticity of demand**)

39. Market supply elasticity measures the producers' supply response to changes in product price. It is calculated as the percentage change in quantity supplied divided by the percentage change in product price. (**Elasticity of supply**)

40. Market supply elasticity is primarily determined by the time needed by a firm to alter production in response to product price changes. Such adjustments will be influenced by:

(a) the availability and prices of resources

(b) the number of producers within an industry

(c) changes in innovations and technology that influence production (**Elasticity of supply**)

41. The shorter the time period in which to alter production, the more inelastic supply is. A crop of oranges is harvested for a specified growing season and brought into the market. This represents a perfectly inelastic market supply condition. A longer time period will allow changes in production, making supply more elastic. (**Elasticity of supply**)

42. An extended time period permits existing firms to alter their inventory of resources and to change their production capacity, and possibly results in the entry of new firms into the industry. All these conditions would contribute to increased market supply elasticity. (**Elasticity of supply**)

Grade Yourself

Circle the numbers of the questions you missed, then fill in the total incorrect for each topic. If you answered more than three questions incorrectly, you need to focus on that topic. (If a topic has less than three questions and you had at least one wrong, we suggest you study that topic also. Read your textbook, or a review book, or ask your teacher for help.)

Subject: Demand and Supply Elasticity

Topic	Question Numbers	Number Incorrect
Elasticity definition	1, 2, 3, 4, 5, 6	
Interpretation of elasticity	7, 8, 9, 10, 11, 12, 13	
Determinants of elasticity	14, 15, 16, 17, 18	
Applications of elasticity	19, 20, 21, 22, 23, 24, 25, 26	
Cross elasticity of demand	27, 28, 29, 30, 31, 32	
Income elasticity of demand	33, 34, 35, 36, 37, 38	
Elasticity of supply	39, 40, 41, 42	

Utility Maximization and Consumer Behavior

4

Test Yourself

1. Define what is meant by a consumer's total utility.

2. How does a consumer's level of total utility change as more units of a product are consumed?

3. Construct a numerical table and illustrate graphically how total utility changes when more units of a product are consumed.

4. Explain the change in total utility from the constructed table.

5. Define and explain marginal utility.

6. What is the relationship between total utility and marginal utility?

7. What is the principle of diminishing marginal utility?

8. How does the principle of diminishing marginal utility relate to the law of demand?

9. What is the relationship between diminishing marginal utility and the elasticity of demand for a product?

10. Explain the principle of utility maximization.

11. Does the principle of utility maximization assume that consumers actually assign numerical values as a measure of the utility they derive from each purchase?

12. What represents an alternative measure of utility or pleasure?

13. Define an indifference curve.

14. Fig. 4a represents an indifference curve of two products, X and Y. Questions 15-18 are based on this graph.

15. What does a movement along an indifference curve represent?

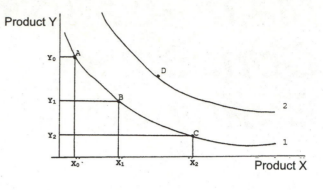

Fig. 4a

16. What is the marginal rate of substitution (MRS)?

17. Examine and explain the movement from Point A to Point C and from Point C to Point A.

18. What does Point D on indifference curve number 2 represent?

19. What is a budget equation?

The graph below is an example of a budget equation assuming products X and Y. Questions 20-24 are based on this graph.

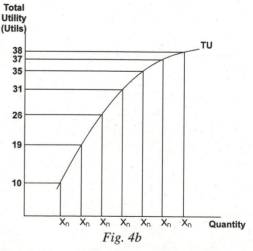

Fig. 4b

20. What does any point on the budget equation represent?

21. Are different amounts of money income being spent at Points A, B, C, or D in this graph? Explain.

22. What does Point E represent?

23. How are changes in product prices represented by the budget equation?

24. Explain the budget equation that is represented by the linear function of A-H.

Questions 25-29 are based on the following indifference curve analysis.

25. Where is consumer behavior maximized under this indifference curves.

26. Discuss utility maximization at Point E.

27. Will the consumer maximize total utility by consuming the quantities of products X and Y represented by Point A? Explain.

28. Does Point B on indifference curve 1 represent utility maximization? Explain.

29. How can the demand curve for a product be constructed with indifference curve analysis?

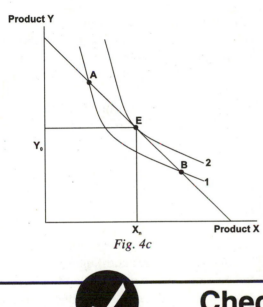

Fig. 4c

✓ Check Yourself

1. Total utility measures a consumer's overall level of satisfaction or pleasure that is derived from the consumption of goods and services. (**Total utility**)

2. Total utility tends to change at a varying rate as more units of a product are consumed. Specifically, total utility tends to increase at a decreasing rate, which means that each additional unit consumed contributes less and less to total utility. (**Total utility**)

3. A numerical example of how total utility changes with increased quantity consensus appears in the table below. This information is shown graphically in Fig. 4.1.

Quantities	Total Utility	
1	10	
2	19	
3	26	
4	31	
5	35	
6	37	
7	38	(**Total utility**)

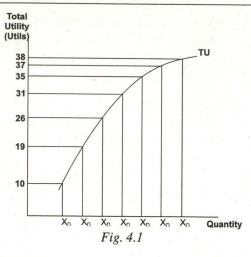

Fig. 4.1

4. The information shows that each additional unit consumed contributes less to the consumer's level of total satisfaction. The first unit contributed 10 utils of satisfaction, the second unit an additional 9 utils, the third unit 7 utils, the fourth 5 utils, the fifth 4 utils, the sixth 2 utils, and the seventh 1 util. Total utility is increasing at a decreasing rate with each additional unit of the product consumed. (**Total utility**)

5. Marginal utility (MU) measures the change in total utility that results from a one unit change in the quantity of the product consumed. From Fig. 4.1 MU per unit consumed decreases as more units are consumed. (**Marginal utility**)

6. Marginal utility is the rate at which total utility changes in response to more or less units of the product being consumed. It is a measure of the slope of the total utility function. Total utility is the sum of marginal utilities to the present consumption level. (**Marginal utility**)

7. The notion of diminishing utility is that total utility will increase at a decreasing rate or that marginal utility decreases as more units of a product are consumed. This means that each additional unit of the product contributes less and less to the consumer's overall satisfaction. The second bottle of soda is less satisfying than the first, and each additional unit will be less satisfying than the previous one consumed. (**Marginal utility**)

8. A consumer is willing to pay only a lower price for additional quantities of a product because their marginal utility of more units is decreasing. In contrast, a consumer will pay a higher price for lesser quantities because the marginal utility of fewer units is higher. This explains the law of demand and the inverse relationship between product price and quantity demanded. (**Marginal utility**)

9. Typically, if additional units of a product consumed have decreases in marginal utility, the demand for the product would tend to be elastic. In contrast, relatively constant marginal utility in response to added consumption would imply a relatively inelastic demand for the product. Thus, decreasing marginal utility implies elastic demand, while constant marginal utility implies inelastic demand. (**Marginal utility**)

10. The principle of utility maximization seeks to explain how consumers would respond within a market setting and buy different products in varied quantities to get the most utility for their money. It suggests that consumers will derive the greatest level of satisfaction if their income is spread over the purchase of various products so that the marginal utility per dollar of the last unit of each product purchased is the same for each product. (**Utility maximization**)

11. The principle of utility maximization assumes that satisfaction can be numerically calculated. This is called cardinal measure, and is not a typical model of consumers' market activity. (**Utility maximization**)

12. All consumers are consciously aware of their likes, preferences, and dislikes. Thus, consumers can prioritize their likes, choices, and preferences as a consumption process. A consumer likes product A more than product B and additionally prefers product B to product C. Thus, it appears that the consumer would prefer product A to product C. In addition, more of something is typically preferred to less. This process of prioritizing consumption behavior is called ordinal measure. It does not seek to quantify or assign numerical values as a measure of consumer satisfaction. (**Utility maximization**)

13. An indifference curve identifies the various combinations of quantities of two products that yield the same level of utility or satisfaction to a consumer. Thus, consumers are indifferent to which combination of products on the curve they actually consume. (**Indifference curve**)

14. Two indifference curves for product X and Y are illustrated in Fig. 4.2. Each of the curves represents various combinations of the two products which yield a certain level of total utility for the consumer. The higher curve shows all the combinations of X and Y that yield a certain level of utility, and the lower curve shows all the combinations of X and Y that yield a lower level of utility. (**Indifference curve**)

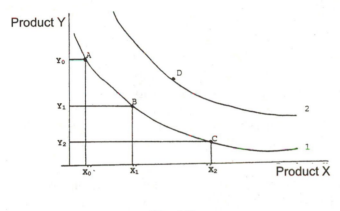

Fig. 4.2

15. A movement from one point to some other point on the indifference curve represents different combinations or quantities of the two products which yield the same level of satisfaction. At Point A the consumer is purchasing a relatively large amount of product Y compared to product X, while at Point C the consumer is purchasing a relatively large portion of product X in comparison to product Y. Both A and C represent the same level of consumer satisfaction. (**Indifference curve**)

16. The marginal rate of substitution is a measure of the slope of the indifference curve and is illustrated as a movement along the function. It measures the rate at which one product is substituted for another along the indifference curve. Its slope is the negative ratio of MU_x to MU_y. (**Indifference curve**)

17. The movement from Point A to Point C on indifference curve 1 illustrates the increased substitution or consumption of product X for product Y at varying rates. As more of product X is consumed, the MU of product X decreases, and the MU of product Y increases as lesser amounts are consumed. Thus, more units of product X must be substituted for units of product Y to maintain the same level of consumer satisfaction or TU at Point A and C. (**Indifference curve**)

In contrast, the movement from Point C to Point A shows more of product Y being purchased and substituted for product X. The MU of product Y decreases as the MU of product X increases. Thus, more of product Y must be substituted for product X to maintain the same level of TU. (**Indifference curve**)

18. Any point on indifference curve 2 represents a greater level of total utility than on indifference curve 1. Thus, Point D represents quantities of product X and Y that would provide the consumer with a greater

level of consumption pleasure that points on A, B, or C. Any movement toward an indifference curve closer to the zero origin would suggest different combinations of the two products that would yield a lesser level of total utility. (**Indifference curve**)

19. The budget equation shows the financial constraints of the consumer's market behavior. (**Budget equation**)

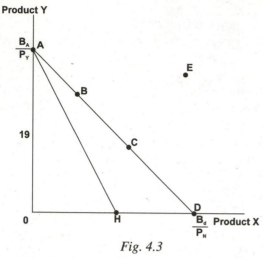

Fig. 4.3

20. A budget equation for products X and Y is illustrated in Fig. 4.3 above. The Y-axis intercept at Point A means that the consumer has spent all of his or her income on the exclusive purchase of product Y. Thus, A is the money budget divided by the price of product Y. The X-axis intercept at Point D shows that the consumer has spent all of his or her income exclusively on purchase of product X. It is calculated as money budget divided by the price of product X.

    Points A, B, C, and D, and any other points on the budget equation, represent the actual numerical amounts or combinations of product X and Y that can be purchased with the consumer's income given the prices of the two products. The slope of the budget equation is measured as the negative ratio of the price of product X to the price of product Y. (**Budget equation**)

21. The amount of money income spent for the different quantities of product X and Y represented by any point on the budget equation is the same. At any point on the budget equation, the consumer's money income has been totally spent. (**Budget equation**)

22. Point E represents a combination of product X and Y that can't be purchased since it is not a point that is on or within the budget line. (**Budget equation**)

23. Changes in product prices are represented by a change in the numerical value of the X or Y axis intercept. An increase in the numerical value of the axis would result from a decrease in price, and a decrease in the numerical value of the axis would confirm an increase in product price. (**Budget equation**)

24. Initially, the budget equation was illustrated as the linear function A-D. Note that point A on the Y-axis intercept didn't change. This means that the price of product Y remained unchanged. However, the X-axis intercept decreased from Point D to Point H. This shows that the selling price of product X increased. (**Budget equation**)

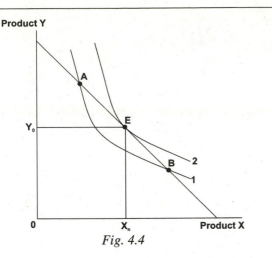

Fig. 4.4

25. With the analysis depicted in Fig. 4.4, consumers will maximize their utility or total satisfaction by purchasing that combination of products X and Y represented by Point E, or OY_o and OX_o. (**Point of tangency**)

26. Point E represents a point of geometric tangency between the budget equation and the indifference curve. This means that their slopes are the same, which then confirms that the MU of the last unit of product Y purchased divided by its price is equal to the MU of the last unit of product X purchased divided by its price. (The Marginal Rate of Substitution is equal to the slope of the Budget Line.)

    At Point E:

    $MU_y/P_y = MU_x/P_x$ (**Point of tangency**)

27. The quantities of products X and Y represented by Point A do not represent utility maximization. Point A, like Point E, confirms that total income has been spent. However, Point A is a combination of both products that represents a lower level of total utility than point E on the higher indifference curve 2. (**Point of tangency**)

28. Similar to combination A, Point B does not represent utility maximization either. All of the consumer's income is spent by purchasing combination B, but the level of utility received is less than that represented by combination E on the higher indifference curve 2. (**Point of tangency**)

29. Each point of utility maximization or tangency such as Point E in Fig. 4.4 (above) represents a coordinate point on the demand curve for the product. It defines a price and quantity relationship. With changes in product prices and new points of tangency within an indifference map, the various coordinate points can be connected to plot the demand curve. (**Point of tangency**)

Grade Yourself

Circle the numbers of the questions you missed, then fill in the total incorrect for each topic. If you answered more than three questions incorrectly, you need to focus on that topic. (If a topic has less than three questions and you had at least one wrong, we suggest you study that topic also. Read your textbook, or a review book, or ask your teacher for help.)

Subject: Utility Maximization and Consumer Behavior

Topic	Question Numbers	Number Incorrect
Total utility	1, 2, 3, 4	
Marginal utility	5, 6, 7, 8, 9	
Utility maximization	10, 11, 12	
Indifference curve	13, 14, 15, 16, 17, 18	
Budget equation	19, 20, 21, 22, 23, 24	
Point of tangency	25, 26, 27, 28, 29, 30	

An Analysis of Production and Costs

5

Production characterizes the relationship between the use of resources, the nature of the manufacturing process, and the output of products within markets. The short-run production period represents the use of both fixed and variable resources, and exhibits the principle of diminishing returns. Fixed costs are generated by the use of fixed resources that do not change during the short-run production period. In contrast, variable resources are alterable, and production in the short run will vary as more or fewer variable quantities of resources are employed within the fixed resource setting.

The level of output will change at a varying rate because of changes in the marginal productivity of the variable resources employed. Costs of production in the short run respond to changes in the level and rates of output. Total costs will increase at a decreasing rate when production increases at an increasing rate. In contrast, total costs will increase at an increasing rate when output is increasing at a decreasing rate.

The long-run production period includes sufficient time in which all resources can be changed. Thus, output will respond to the increased or lessened use of the entire resource base and exhibit economies or diseconomies of scale. Increasing rates imply decreasing costs of production.

Explicit costs are recordable or accountable expenses incurred in the production process. In contrast, implicit costs can be equated with opportunity costs and alternative uses that may be made of resources within markets. They represent a necessary return to justify the riskful uncertainty of a given investment and production decision.

Test Yourself

1. What are explicit costs of production?

2. What are implicit costs of production?

3. What are normal profits for a business?

4. What are economic profits for a business?

5. Define the short-run production period.

6. What characterizes the short-run production period?

7. What is the marginal physical product of a variable resource?

8. Explain the Law of Diminishing Returns and discuss how MPP changes in the short run.

Quantities of Labor	Total Output	MPP_L	APP_L
1	5	5	5.0
2	15	10	7.5
3	30	15	10.0
4	42	12	10.5
5	45	7	9.0
6	45	0	7.5

Table 5.1

9. What is average physical product or APP?

10. From the information in Table 5.1 above, plot the total output curve.

11. From the information in Table 5.1, plot the MPP and APP functions and explain the relationship between total output, MPP, and APP.

12. What is the relationship between MPP and APP?

13. Define fixed and variable costs.

14. Illustrate graphically the nature of variable, fixed, and total costs.

15. Define average fixed costs, average variable costs, and average costs.

16. Illustrate graphically the nature of AFC, AVC, and AC.

17. Assume that the total cost function for a product is expressed as: $TC = 10 + 5Q$. Calculate the elements of cost and output equal to 10 units.

18. Define marginal cost of production.

19. What determines the nature of short-run cost conditions?

20. Describe the production and cost relationship in the short run.

21. What is the relationship between APP and AC in the short run?

22. What is the notion of loss minimization?

23. What is a simple example of loss minimization?

24. What is the long-run production period?

25. What characterizes long-run production and costs?

26. Explain how the long-run average cost function of a firm is derived?

27. Explain what is meant by economies of scale.

28. What conditions might contribute to increased economies of scale?

29. Explain what is meant by diseconomies of scale.

30. What conditions might contribute to diseconomies of scale?

The following graph illustrates the relationship between economies and diseconomies of scale to the long-run average cost function. Questions 31-33 are based on this illustration.

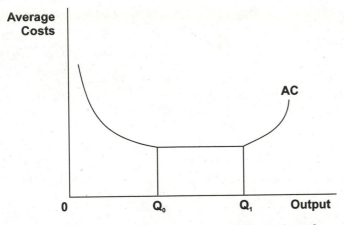

31. Within what range of output are economies of scale represented in this figure?

32. Within what range of output are diseconomies of scale represented?

33. What is represented within the output range from Q_0 - Q_1?

34. What are external economies and diseconomies of scale?

35. What is the impact of an external economy of scale?

36. What might be examples of external economies of scale?

37. What is the impact of an external diseconomy of scale?

38. What are possible examples of external diseconomies of scale?

39. What determines a firm's long-run cost curves?

Check Yourself

1. Explicit costs are recorded and accountable money expenses incurred in the business operation, whether it is involved in the production of products or the rendering of services. Payments for the use of all resources used would be examples of explicit costs. (**Economic costs and profits**)

2. Implicit costs represent opportunity costs and alternative uses for various capital investment and production choices. They are a measure of the risk and uncertainty of a specific investment choice and must be covered to justify continuation of operations. (**Economic costs and profits**)

3. Normal profits represent a financial return from production and sales that covers the firm's average costs of production, which consist of both implicit and explicit costs. Normal profits mean that total revenue equals total costs (TR = TC), or that price equals average costs of production (P = AC). (**Economic costs and profits**)

4. Economic profits exist when the level of total revenue exceeds total costs (TR > TC), or when price exceeds average costs of production (P > AC). (**Economic costs and profits**)

5. Fixed and variable resources are employed during the short-run production period. It is a limited period that does not permit a business to alter its fixed resource base. Thus, production is increased or decreased in response to the greater or lesser use of variable resources on the fixed resource base. (**Short-run period**)

6. The short-run production period is characterized by the Law of Diminishing Returns. This means that output will change at a varying rate as a result of the marginal productivity of the variable resource. (**Short-run period**)

7. The marginal physical product (MPP) of a variable resource measures the incremental or individual contribution of each unit of the employed variable resource to the production process. (**Short-run period**)

8. Changes in the MPP of the variable resource determine how production changes. This is illustrated in Table 5.1. Initially, the MPP of the first three units of the variable resource (labor) increases. Each unit contributes more than the previous unit, which means that total output is increasing at a greater or increasing rate. Thus, production increases at an increasing rate when MPP is rising. However, the MPP decreases for the fourth, fifth, and sixth units of labor, which means that output will increase at a lower or decreasing rate until it reaches its maximum level of 45 units. (**Short run**)

9. The average physical product (APP) of the variable resource is measured as the ratio or proportion of output at each level of variable resource use. The APP of the first unit is 5, the second, 7.5, and the third, 10. It then decreases as a result of the decrease in the MPP of the variable resource. (**Short run**)

10. The graphed total output from the data in Table 5.1 appears in Fig. 5.1. Its slope at various levels of total output conforms to the Law of Diminishing Returns and is a measure of the MPP of the variable resource. (**Short run**)

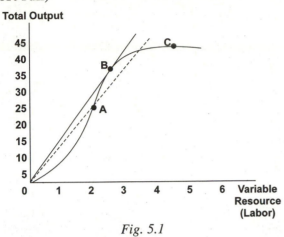

Fig. 5.1

11. The graphed MPP and APP functions from the data in Table 5.1 appear in Fig. 5.2. The MPP of labor initially increases and reaches its maximum value when the third unit of labor is employed, which corresponds to an output level of 30 units. Represented by the point of inflection (A) on the total output curve, this corresponds to maximum MPP at point A′ in Figure 5.2. MPP then decreases as additional units of labor are employed, which results in smaller increases in output. APP will increase and be greatest when the fourth unit of labor is employed. Represented by the point of tangency of the ray OB and the total output curve, this corresponds to maximum APP at point B′ in Figure 5.2. Thereafter APP begins to decrease. (**Short run**)

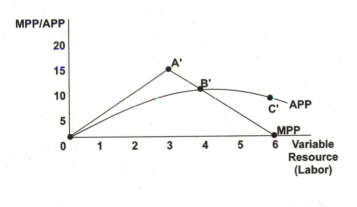

Fig. 5.2

12. When MPP exceeds APP, then APP is rising, and it will decrease when MPP is below and falling. That means that the MPP curve will intersect APP at its maximum value. (**Short run**)

13. Fixed costs are associated with the use of fixed resources in production and remain unchanged over all levels of short-run production. In contrast, variable costs are associated with the use of variable resources and change as more or fewer units are employed. (**Short-run costs**)

14. Fixed, variable, and total costs are illustrated in Fig. 5.3. The fixed cost function is a horizontal line parallel to the X-axis that confirms that fixed costs remain unchanged over all levels of output. The curvature of the variable and total cost functions are determined by diminishing returns in the short run. **(Short-run costs)**

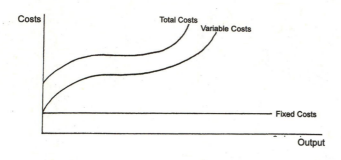

Fig. 5.3

15. Average fixed cost is fixed cost per unit of output, or:

AFC = FC/Q.

Average variable cost is average cost per unit of output, or: AVC = VC/Q.

Average cost is total cost per unit of output, or:

AC = TC/Q = AFC + AVC. **(Short-run costs)**

16. AFC, AVC, and AC are illustrated in Fig. 5.4. The AFC curve decreases as output increases, and the AVC and AC curves are the result of the Law of Diminishing Returns. Note that the AC and AVC curves approach each other as output is increased because AFC continually lessens. **(Short-run costs)**

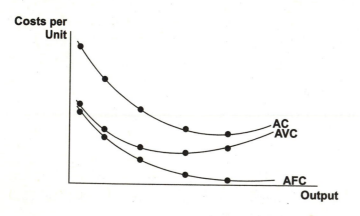

Fig. 5.4

17. In the total cost function: TC = 10 + 5 Q, the value 10 represents fixed costs, and variable costs are expressed as 5Q. Thus, when the level of output is 10 units, the different levels of cost are:

FC = 10 and AFC = FC/Q = 10/10 = 1

VC = 5 x 10 = 50 and AVC = VC/Q = 50/10 = 5

TC = 10 + 50 = 60 and AC = TC/Q = 60/10 = 6 or AC = AFC + AVC = 1 + 5 = 6 **(Short-run costs)**

18. Marginal cost (MC) measures the change in total costs that results from a change in the level of output. It is calculated as: $MC = \Delta TC / \Delta Q$.

    If total costs increase from 100 to 105 as the additional tenth unit is produced, then the MC of the tenth unit of output is 5. MC is also a measure of the slopes of a firm's total cost curve. (**Short-run costs**)

19. Since the Law of Diminishing Returns affects short-run production, it also determines the nature of cost conditions in the short run. In short, there exists an inverse symmetrical relationship between changes in production and corresponding changes in costs because of diminishing returns. (**Production and costs**)

20. Production increases at an increasing rate when MPP is increasing. This means that MC is decreasing and total costs are increasing at a decreasing rate. Production will then increase at a decreasing rate when MPP is decreasing. This means that total costs are increasing at an increasing rate and MC is rising. (**Production and costs**)

21. The relationship between APP and AC is determined by the Law of Diminishing Returns. AC is falling when APP is rising, and AC is rising when APP is decreasing. The MPP curve intersects APP from above at its maximum point, and the MC curve intersects RC from below at its minimum point. (**Production and costs**)

22. The notion of loss minimization suggests that a firm can actually minimize its loss where revenues are less than total costs by continuing in production. A firm must at least cover all variable costs that are incurred because of the discretionary decision to produce. If it can additionally cover some of its fixed costs, then its actual loss is less than if it terminates production and incurs a loss equal to total fixed costs. (**Production and costs**)

23. The firm is producing and selling ten units of output at a price of ninety cents. Its total revenue is nine dollars. Its AVC is sixty cents so total VC is six dollars. In addition, its AFC is forty cents, so its FC is four dollars. The firm's total cost of producing ten units of output is ten dollars, and with revenues of nine dollars, its net loss is one dollar. If it terminates production, its total loss would be all of its fixed costs of four dollars. Thus, it minimizes its loss by continuing to produce. (**Production and costs**)

24. The long-run production period varies among firms and depends upon the type of product being produced and the production process itself. It represents a sufficient period of time in which all resources are variable. Thus, the firm can change production by using more or less of the entire variable resource base. (**Long run**)

25. Long-run production and costs are characterized by economies or diseconomies of scale. They represent how production changes in response to changes in the use of variable resources. (**Long run**)

26. The long-run average cost curve consists of appropriate segments of short-run cost functions that represent various levels of productive capacity for the firm. Any point on the long-run average cost curve represents least cost production for that level of output. (**Long run**)

27. Economies of scale represent cost-saving benefits that accrue to a firm from expanded production. It means that output increases at a greater rate than the increased cost of using more variable resources in production. Thus, the firm's AC decrease, and this condition is commonly called increasing returns and decreasing costs. (**Long run**)

28. Many factors can generate favorable economies of scale that result in decreasing cost conditions. They might result from: the introduction of new production technology or new work-related innovations, increased employee training, redesigning task flows, increased use of specialized labor and other resources, etc. (**Long run**)

29. Diseconomies of scale represent internal cost inefficiencies for the firm that result in rising unit costs of production. Consequently, production increases at lower rates as more units of the variable resources are employed. Thus, the firm's AC increase, and the condition is commonly called decreasing returns and increasing costs. (**Long run**)

30. Many conditions that are uniquely internal to the firm may result in diseconomies of scale. Some of the conditions may include failure of adequate communication between management and unions that results in apathy towards work and a poor working environment, lack of cost-efficient equipment and other capital products, etc. (**Long run**)

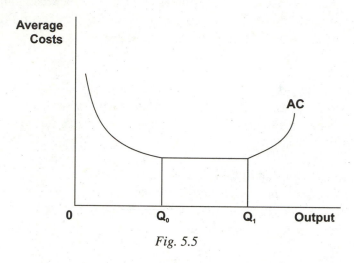

Fig. 5.5

31. The illustration in Fig. 5.5 exhibits the relationship between economies and diseconomies scale and the long-run AC curve.

    Economies of scale are represented within the output range of OQ_0. As production increases, the firm's AC decrease. Thus, the firm is incurring decreasing costs and increasing returns. (**Economies and diseconomies of scale**)

32. Diseconomies of scale are represented beyond the output range of OQ_1. As production increases, the firm's AC increase. Thus, the firm is incurring increasing costs and decreasing returns. (**Economies and diseconomies of scale**)

33. Constant returns and constant costs characterize the production range between Q_0 and Q_1. This means that total costs change by the same amount with each additional unit of output, so that the firm's average costs of production remain unchanged. Any change in the level of output within this production range will not alter the firm's AC. (**Economies and diseconomies of scale**)

34. External economies and diseconomies of scale are conditions that impact upon a firm's production costs. However, they are removed from or are imposed upon the firm, which has no control over their impact upon its cost conditions. (**Economies and diseconomies of scale**)

35. An external economy of scale will favorably affect the firm by reducing its average costs of production at all levels of output. It is exhibited as a parallel downward shift in the firm's AC curve. As a result, AC at all levels of output decrease. (**Economies and diseconomies of scale**)

36. These are conditions that lower the firm's operational costs and are removed from or independent of the firm's decisions and operations. Examples might include government deregulation, the ineffectiveness of OPEC, which lessens oil and energy prices, a nation's immigration policies that impact upon domestic labor supply, and others. (**Economies and diseconomies of scale**)

37. An external diseconomy of scale will unfavorably affect the firm by increasing its average costs of production at all levels of output. It is exhibited as a parallel upward shift in the firm's AC curve. As a result, AC increase at all levels of output. (**Economies and diseconomies of scale**)

38. These conditions increase the firm's costs of production and are independent of any of the firm's decisions or operations. Examples would include the costly imposition of more government regulations, taxes, political unrest in foreign nations that are major resource markets, natural disasters that impact upon the availability of resources, etc. (**Economies and diseconomies of scale**)

39. A firm's long-run cost functions are determined by economies and diseconomies of scale. The slope or curvature of the long-run cost functions depends upon internal economies and diseconomies of scale, whereas the location of the function depends upon external economies and diseconomies of scale. (**Economies and diseconomies of scale**)

Grade Yourself

Circle the numbers of the questions you missed, then fill in the total incorrect for each topic. If you answered more than three questions incorrectly, you need to focus on that topic. (If a topic has less than three questions and you had at least one wrong, we suggest you study that topic also. Read your textbook, or a review book, or ask your teacher for help.)

Subject: An Analysis of Production and Costs

Topic	Question Numbers	Number Incorrect
Economic costs and profits	1, 2, 3, 4	
Short-run period	5, 6, 7	
Short run	8, 9, 10, 11, 12	
Short-run costs	13, 14, 15, 16, 17, 18	
Production and costs	19, 20, 21, 22, 23	
Long run	24, 25, 26, 27, 28, 29, 30	
Economies and diseconomies of scale	31, 32, 33, 34, 35, 36, 37, 38, 39	

The Purely Competitive Market Structure

6

Brief Yourself

Pure competition is an important type of market structure. Capitalism as an economic system and the allocative and distributive functions of the market process are dependent upon competition. The justification for government to evolve and enforce regulatory policies is based upon the benefits that are associated with competitive industries.

The noted characteristics of a purely competitive industry include the existence of a large number of rival firms, each producing standardized products; determination of product prices by market indications; and the ability of each competitive firm to sell all of its output at market-determined price. In addition, firms within a purely competitive industry don't exert any discretionary control over their product markets, and barriers to entry or exit are not prohibitive. This means that it is relatively easy for new firms to enter the industry and that firms can also discontinue operations and exit the industry with minimal loss.

The purely competitive industry exhibits long-run market adjustments that ensure that firms earn a normal profit. This confirms that products are being produced at lowest cost and that consumers pay a product price that approximates the minimum cost of production and distribution. It is an ideal market standard by which other types of industries are evaluated.

Test Yourself

1. What are the four different types of market structures?

2. What are some of the differences that contribute to these different market structures?

3. What are the dominant characteristics of the purely competitive market structure?

4. Why is it important for a large number of firms to exist within the industry?

5. What is the result of standardized production by purely competitive firms?

6. Does the high degree of product substitutability impact upon the price elasticity of demand for the products?

7. How does perfect price elasticity of demand relate to the "price-taker" characteristic of purely competitive firms?

8. What is the relationship between price and

marginal revenue for purely competitive firms?

9. Define marginal revenue and discuss its relationship to the firm's total revenue for a firm within a purely competitive market.

10. Illustrate the "price-taker" characteristic of the purely competitive firm and its relationship to demand and marginal revenue.

11. What are barriers to entry?

12. What is meant by non-prohibitive barriers to entry for a purely competitive industry?

13. How do long-run adjustments occur within the purely competitive industry?

14. What occurs in the long run when short-run economic profits exist?

15. What is the amount of economic profit that the representative firm is earning before the long-run adjustments?

16. What are the firm's profits after the long-run adjustments?

17. What occurs in the long run when short-run industry losses exist?

18. What is particularly ideal about the long-run price within a purely competitive industry?

19. What does that condition imply about resource allocation and the interests of consumers?

20. Is this long-run norm approximated within any other type of market structure?

21. What is profit maximization?

22. How much of the product should be produced to maximize profits?

23. Illustrate an example of profit maximization.

24. Under what production and cost conditions should a firm terminate its operations?

25. What is the relationship between a firm's MC and short-run supply?

26. Illustrate an increasing-cost long-run supply curve for a purely competitive firm.

27. Illustrate a decreasing-cost long-run supply curve for a purely competitive firm.

28. Illustrate a constant-cost long-run supply curve for a purely competitive firm.

29. Why is the purely competitive model important to a capitalist economy system?

30. What are examples of market failures?

31. What are externalities or external costs?

32. Are there any significant examples of pure competition within the economy?

✓ Check Yourself

1. The four types of market models consist of:

   a. pure competition

   b. monopolistic competition

   c. oligopoly

   d. pure monopoly (**Market structures**)

2. These four different types of market structures may exhibit differences in the products being produced, the resource requirements needed in production, the types of markets that they seek to serve, their costs, and the selling prices of their products. (**Market structures**)

3. The noted characteristics of pure competition include:

   a. the existence of a large number of firms within the industry

   b. absence of control over price, so that individual firms are price-takers

   c. complete standardization of the products produced

   d. absence of prohibitively high barriers to entry or exit

   e. long-run market adjustments characteristic of the industry (**Pure competition**)

4. The large number of firms that characterize purely competitive industry means that no one firm or select few are able to distort, control, or manipulate market supply. Each firm produces a limited and small share of total industry supply. (**Pure competition**)

5. The standardized products of purely competitive firms allow consumers to readily substitute the products in consumption. There are no distinctive features that differentiate the products and any one firm, and consumers do not develop any brand loyalty. (**Pure competition**)

6. The demand for an individual firm's product within a purely competitive industry is considered to be perfectly elastic in nature. Thus, the demand curve is illustrated as a linear function horizontal to the X-axis. (**Pure competition**)

7. The demand function is also the purely competitive firm's price schedule. This product price is the market-determined price at which all the firms sell their output. (**Pure competition**)

8. Since the selling price of the product is constant, the firm's total revenue increases in response to changes in the level of sales. This means that the firm's marginal revenue equals price and remains constant at all levels of output and sales. (**Pure competition**)

9. Marginal revenue (MR) measures the change in a firm's total revenue that results from changes in the level of output and sales. It is a measure of the slope of the total revenue function. (**Pure competition**)

10. Market demand and supply determine the equilibrium. The individual firm and all firms within the purely competitive industry sell their output at the market price. The price schedule is simultaneously the firm's demand and MR function. (**Pure competition**)

11. Barriers to entry are various impediments or constraints that limit the ability of potential new firms to enter an industry. They may be product related, market features, or technological and financial requirements needed to begin operations. (**Pure competition**)

12. Barriers are not prohibitive within a purely competitive industry. This means that new firms can enter the industry and begin operations with relative ease. Conversely, if conditions within the industry are not profitable, it is relatively easy for firms to terminate operations and exit from the industry. (**Pure competition**)

13. The long-run adjustment process within the purely competitive industry takes place through the entry or exit of firms, the resulting change in market supply, and its impact upon long-run market price. Another source of long-run adjustment is technological advance. (**Long-run adjustment**)

14. This long-run adjustment process is illustrated in Fig. 6.2. The representative firm is initially earning an economic profit at the market price of OP (determined by the intersection of S and D at Point X). This attracts additional firms into the industry and market supply expands to S_1 which decreases the new long-run market price OP_1 (corresponding to Point Y). At this lower price the firm is now earning a normal profit. (**Long-run adjustment**)

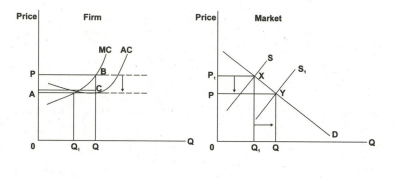

Fig. 6.2

15. The firm's short-run economic profits are AP per unit, and its total economic profits are APBC. (**Long-run adjustment**)

16. The new long-run market price is OP_1 or OA for the individual firm. Price equals marginal revenue, marginal cost, and minimum average cost. The firm is earning a normal profit. (**Long-run adjustment**)

17. This long-run adjustment process is illustrated in Fig. 6.3. The initial market price is OP, which is less than the firm's level of average costs at the output level of OQ. The firm's unit loss is PA, and its total losses at output level Q are PABC. These losses result in the shutdown of some industry firms and their exit from the industry. The result is a decrease in market supply to S_1 and an increase in market price to OP_1. For the individual firm, the new long-run price is OA, which equals its average costs. Thus, in the long run the purely competitive firm is has a normal profit. (**Long-run adjustment**)

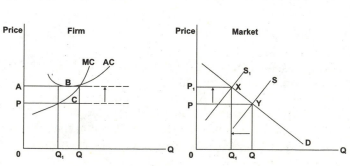

Fig. 6.3

18. The long-run price within a purely competitive market will equal the firm's marginal revenue, its marginal cost, and its minimum average costs of production. (**Long-run adjustment**)

19. The long-run purely competitive norm is ideal since it implies that resources are most efficiently being allocated into production under lower cost conditions. Moreover, the interests of consumers are optimized since the product's selling price equals lower cost. (**Long-run adjustment**)

20. It is only within the purely competitive model that $P = MR = MC = $ minimum AC. (**Long-run adjustment**)

21. Profit maximization represents a level of output where profits per unit of output and sale are greatest. The margin or the difference between revenue and cost is greatest with profit maximization. (**Profit maximization**)

22. A firm will maximize its total profits when it produces and sells a level of output where marginal revenue (MR) is equal to marginal cost (MC). (**Profit maximization**)

23. Profit maximization is illustrated in Fig. 6.4 at output level Q_p. The slope of the total revenue curve is MR, and the slope of the total cost curve is MC. The TR curve and the straight line that is tangent to the TC curve are parallel, which means that their respective slopes, or MR and MC, are equal. Thus, at output level OQ_p, the difference between TR and TC is greatest. Thus, economic profits are greatest at that level of output. (**Profit maximization**)

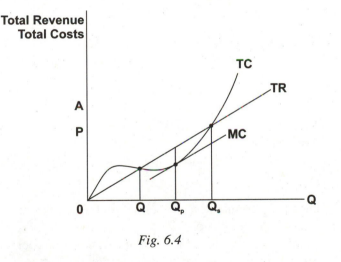

Fig. 6.4

24. A firm will minimize its losses if its revenues cover all of its variable costs and a portion of its fixed costs. It should terminate production if its revenues are insufficient to cover all of its variable costs. (**Loss minimization**)

25. The firm's short-run supply curve represents that portion of its MC function that lies above minimum average variable costs. This condition confirms that it is covering all of its variable costs and an increasing portion of its fixed costs. Thus, it will minimize its losses by continuing to produce. (**Loss minimization**)

26. The long-run supply function S_i in Fig. 6.5 exhibits increasing cost conditions. It is positively sloped, and there is a direct relationship between changes in output and resulting changes in average costs. (**Long-run supply**)

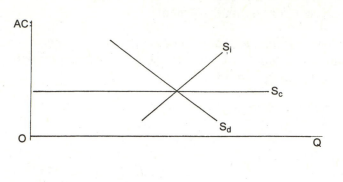

Fig. 6.5

27. The long-run supply function S_d in Fig. 6.5 shows decreasing costs. It is negatively sloped, and there is an inverse relationship between changes in output and resulting changes in average cost. (**Long-run supply**)

28. The long-run supply function S_c in Fig. 6.5 shows constant cost conditions. Unit or average costs remain constant at any level or change in output. (**Long-run supply**)

29. A capitalist economic system relies upon functioning markets to allocate resources into production and distribute products into consumption. Pure competition must exist to ensure that the markets are not manipulated or distorted. (**Pure competition and capitalism**)

30. Non-competitive market conditions might result in the manipulation of supply by a select few large firms impacting upon market prices and be detrimental to the interests of consumers. (**Pure competition and capitalism**)

31. Externalities represent conditions that spill over from the market process. They are external costs or benefits that are borne by the entire society. The environmental decay equated with industrialization and the cost to society of correcting the condition are examples of externalities and external costs. The increased health of society resulting from government-sponsored immunizations is an example of external benefits. (**Pure competition and capitalism**)

32. There are no significant large-scale examples of the purely competitive model within the economy. The agricultural sector has been historically cited as an example of an approximate purely competitive condition, but current successful farming requires high capitalization. As a result, it is now commonly called *agri-business*, which means that a limited number of large producers exist within the industry. The purely competitive norm may be approximated on a limited basis within regional or local markets. (**Pure competition and capitalism**)

Grade Yourself

Circle the numbers of the questions you missed, then fill in the total incorrect for each topic. If you answered more than three questions incorrectly, you need to focus on that topic. (If a topic has less than three questions and you had at least one wrong, we suggest you study that topic also. Read your textbook, or a review book, or ask your teacher for help.)

Subject: The Purely Competitive Market Structure

Topic	Question Numbers	Number Incorrect
Market structure	1, 2	
Pure competition	3, 4, 5, 6, 7, 8, 9, 10, 11, 12	
Long-range adjustment	13, 14, 15, 16, 17, 18, 19, 20	
Profit maximization	21, 22, 23	
Loss minimization	24, 25	
Long-run supply	26, 27, 28	
Pure competition and capitalism	29, 30, 31, 32	

The Pure Monopoly and Monopolistically Competitive Market Structures

7

Brief Yourself

The pure monopoly market structure shows a striking contrast to the purely competitive model. It is a market setting in which one firm accounts for total market supply, there are no ready substitute products available to consumers, and barriers to entry are prohibitively high. Various market and product characteristics make it impossible for new firms to successfully attempt to enter the industry. Without competition, the purely monopolistic firm has exclusive control over its product quantity and may be able to earn both short- and long-run economic profits.

A pure monopoly market condition is generally illegal in the private sector of the economy. The nation's regulatory policies seek to promote and preserve competitive markets by declaring monopoly power illegal.

In contrast, the pure monopoly structure is legally encouraged and permitted within the public or regulated sectors of the economy. The pure monopoly firm is declared a "natural monopoly" and permitted to be the sole producer or supplier of products or services within specific geographical markets. Unique market demand and cost conditions justify these regulatory policies. Within these regulated "natural monopoly" markets, government policies shape the firm's production or service capacity, quality, and the price paid by the consumer.

Monopolistic competition characterizes industrial markets with a large number of relatively small-sized firms that are producing differentiated products. Consumers identify with specific products, and product demand is more inelastic in nature than in pure competition. This permits the firms to maintain some degree of control over product prices, a strikingly different situation from that of a purely competitive market.

Test Yourself

1. What is a pure monopoly market structure?

2. Are there a large number of substitute products available to the consumer within a pure monopoly?

3. Are product prices market-determined within a market structure of pure monopoly?

4. Is it difficult for new firms to enter a market setting of pure monopoly?

5. What are the legal implications of pure monopoly?

6. What product and market conditions might contribute to prohibitive barriers to entry?

7. What is the difference in the market demand function for a purely competitive firm and a pure monopoly?

8. What are the implications of a downsloping demand curve for a pure monopoly?

9. What are the price and production policies used by a pure monopoly?

10. Show a graphic example in which a pure monopolist is incurring an economic profit.

11. Will these economic profits result in a long-run adjustment in which they are eliminated?

12. Illustrate an example in which a pure monopoly firm is incurring an economic loss.

13. Will these economic losses result in a long-run adjustment in which the losses are eliminated?

14. Are the market results of a pure monopoly similar to those of a purely competitive firm?

15. Since a pure monopoly can control production price, is it able to charge different customers different prices?

16. Are pure monopolists permitted to engage in price discrimination?

17. While illegal in the private sectors of the economy, can "natural monopolies" engage in price discrimination in the regulated sectors?

18. What demand considerations are important for "natural monopoly" industries?

19. What unique cost considerations justify the existence of "natural monopoly" industries?

20. What considerations are important in determining the price of a natural monopoly?

21. What is the basis for price discrimination or peak-load pricing within the regulated markets of a natural monopoly?

22. What are monopolistically competitive industries?

23. Is it probable for one firm or a select few large firms to dominate markets?

24. Are barriers to entry considered to be prohibitively high within monopolistically competitive industries?

25. What is product differentiation?

26. What is the impact of product differentiation?

27. What conditions contribute to product differentiation?

28. Can product differentiation contribute to barriers to entry?

29. Illustrate a monopolistically competitive firm incurring an economic profit in the short run.

30. What is the impact of short-run economic profits within monopolistically competitive industry?

31. Illustrate a monopolistically competitive firm incurring an economic loss in the short run.

32. What is the impact of short-run economic losses upon monopolistically competitive industry in the long run?

33. What is meant by the "wastes of monopolistic competition"?

34. Illustrate the differences between a purely competitive and a monopolistically competitive firm in the long run.

35. Are both firms incurring a normal profit in the long run?

36. What are the differences between both firms in the long run?

37. Does a monopolistically competitive firm achieve allocative efficiency in the long run?

38. Does a monopolistically competitive firm maximize the ideal interests of consumers?

39. What criticisms are commonly directed towards advertising?

40. What argument does advertising present in its defense?

✓ Check Yourself

1. A pure monopoly market structure exists when only one firm produces the product. There are no additional firms in the industry. The one firm constitutes the entire industry. (**Pure monopoly**)

2. Immediate substitute products are not available to consumers. There are no rival firms producing products that can be substituted for the pure monopolist's product. (**Pure monopoly**)

3. Product prices are not market-determined under conditions of pure monopoly. The pure monopolist is the sole producer within the market and is able to set the quantity available to consumers. Pure monopolists have total pricing control over their markets. (**Pure monopoly**)

4. Barriers to entry are prohibitively high within pure monopoly markets. Product and market conditions make it extremely difficult or impossible for new firms to enter the industry. (**Pure monopoly**)

5. Pure monopoly is generally illegal within the private sectors of the economy. In contrast, "natural monopolies" are permissible within the public or regulated sectors of the economy. (**Pure monopoly**)

6. Varying conditions contribute to high barriers to entry. A pure monopoly firm may have exclusive control over resources, and the capitalization requirements to initiate operations may be excessive. Additionally, a firm's exclusive patent control over technology may exclude potential competitors from the industry. (**Pure monopoly**)

7. The demand curve for a purely competitive firm is perfectly elastic in nature. The demand curve for the pure monopoly is the industry demand curve and is downsloping. (**Pure monopoly**)

8. The pure monopolist's downsloping demand curve means that it must lower the product price to increase sales. This results in marginal revenue being less than price at all levels of output. (**Pure monopoly**)

9. The pure monopolist will seek to maximize profits and produce that level of output where MR equals MC. (**Price, profits, and costs**)

10. The pure monopoly firm in Fig. 7.1 is incurring unit economic profits of AP. That is the difference between price and average costs at output level OQ. Total economic profits are APBC. (**Price, profits, and costs**)

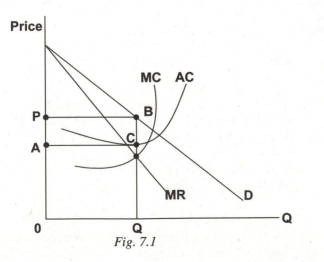

Fig. 7.1

11. Unlike a purely competitive industry, additional firms will not enter a pure monopoly market in the long run. Thus, the firm will likely continue to earn economic profits in the long run. (**Prices, profits, and costs**)

12. Fig. 7.2 illustrates a pure monopolist that is incurring economic losses. The firm will produce quantity OQ where MR equals MC, and charge a price of OP. At that level of output the firm's average costs are OA. Thus, the firm's unit loss is PA and its total economic losses are PABC. (**Prices, profits, and costs**)

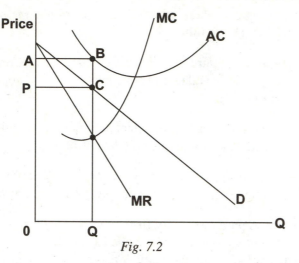

Fig. 7.2

13. The economic losses will be eliminated if the firm elects to terminate operations or decides to continue operations with a loss minimization strategy. The latter means that it continues to produce at a loss as long as its revenues cover all variable costs and a portion of fixed costs. However, production cannot continue indefinitely. (**Prices, profits, and costs**)

14. A purely competitive firm will approximate efficient lowest-cost production and product price. These market conditions are not typically approximated under pure monopoly. Rather, both production and consumption are likely to be less, and the product price will be higher. (**Prices, profits, and costs**)

15. With its control a pure monopolist can potentially charge different prices to different customers in different markets. This is called price discrimination. (**Price discrimination**)

16. Antitrust policies prohibit price discrimination unless:

    a. different quantities are purchased, justifying quantity discounts and price differences;

    b. there are quality differences in the products sold to different customers;

    c. there are transportation cost differences in selling to customers in different geographical markets. (**Price discrimination**)

17. Price discrimination is permitted within the regulated sectors of the economy. For example, the "natural monopoly" firms are allowed to charge different prices to different customers at different hours of a day and days of the week. This is often called peak-load pricing. (**Price discrimination**)

18. Natural monopolies provide critical and indispensable services or products that are necessary for all consumers. The demand for these services is very inelastic and provides the justification for regulation of the firm by government. (**Natural monopoly**)

19. For various reasons, natural monopolies tend to experience decreasing cost conditions over an extended range of output. Thus, it is preferable to permit one firm to expand production to meet optimal demand while incurring lower and lower costs of production. (**Natural monopoly**)

20. The government-regulated price must cover the natural monopolist's explicit costs of production. In addition, because such firms are privately owned and must attract investors' capital, the price must also cover implicit costs and provide the firm with a competitive and fair return. (**Natural monopoly**)

21. The regulated natural monopoly may experience rising unit costs during non-peak demand periods. To moderate these cost inefficiencies, the discounted price seeks to offset the expected decrease in demand with the reduced off-peak prices. These prices often approximate the firm's marginal costs. (**Natural monopoly**)

22. Monopolistic competition is characterized by industrial structures with a large number of relatively small-sized firms that are producing differentiated products. (**Monopolistic competition**)

23. Each monopolistically competitive firm produces and sells a limited and small portion of total industry output. Consequently, such firms do not control market supply or other industry conditions. (**Monopolistic competition**)

24. Barriers to entry are relatively low within monopolistically competitive industries. However, effective product differentiation does contribute to entry constraints for new firms within the industry. (**Monopolistic competition**)

25. Product differentiation means that consumers distinguish among the products of the different producers. (**Product differentiation**)

26. Product differentiation reduces the degree of substitutability among products from the same industry. Consumers identify with a certain product and will only buy that product. This makes the demand for the product more inelastic in nature. (**Product differentiation**)

27. Advertising often creates perceived differentiation, as do real differences among the products. Examples include differences in quality, function, durability, warranty, packaging, and others. (**Product differentiation**)

28. Product differentiation that successfully reduces substitutability can be a prohibitive barrier to entry. New firms may not be able to successfully enter new markets because of consumer allegiance to a specific product, brand, or trademark. (**Product differentiation**)

29. An example of a monopolistically competitive firm incurring an economic profit is shown in Fig. 7.3. The profit maximizing level of output (where MR = MC) is OQ. At that output level, the firm's unit economic profit is AP, and total economic profits are APBC. (**Profits and losses**)

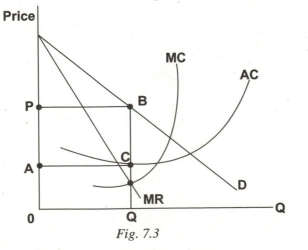

Fig. 7.3

30. Short-run economic profits will result in new firms entering the industry. As a result, it is assumed that monopolistically competitive firms incur only a normal profit in the long run. **(Profits and losses)**

31. An example of a monopolistically competitive firm incurring a short-run economic loss is illustrated in Fig. 7.4. The product selling price is OP, and the firm's average costs at output level OQ are OA. Thus, the unit economic loss is P-A, and total economic losses are PABC. **(Profits and losses)**

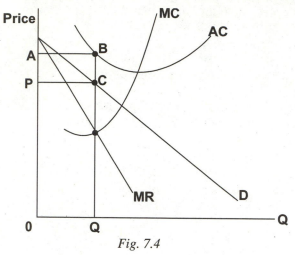

Fig. 7.4

32. The existence of economic losses will result in firms exiting from the industry, and market supply will decrease. Thus, the long-run adjusted price will ensure that all firms earn a normal profit at which price equals average costs. **(Profits and losses)**

33. The phrase "the wastes of monopolistic competition" refers to the striking market contrasts between purely competitive and monopolistically competitive industries. **(Wastes of monopolistic competition)**

34. The long-run differences among the two industries is illustrated in Fig. 7.5. The long-run break-even market solution for a monopolistically competitive firm is approximated at E_m where the quantity demand equals OQ_m at price OP_m. The long-run market solution for a pure competitive firm is approximated at E_c where quantity demanded equals OQ_c. At E_c, the firm's price equals MC and minimum AC. **(Wastes of monopolistic competition)**

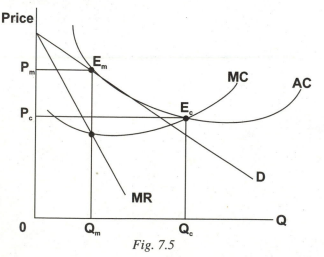

Fig. 7.5

35. Both the pure and monopolistically competitive firms are incurring normal profits in the long run. The monopolistically competitive firm's long-run price is OP_m, which equals AC. The purely competitive firm's long-run price is OP_c, which also equals AC. (**Wastes of monopolistic competition**)

36. The monopolistically competitive firm's output of OQ_m is less than the purely competitive firm's level of output of OQ_c. This results in high long-run prices for monopolistically competitive firms. These differences in output and prices are called "the wastes of monopolistic competition." (**Wastes of monopolistic competition**)

37. The monopolistically competitive firm does not achieve long-run allocative efficiency because the firm is not producing at minimum average costs of production, as realized in a purely competitive market setting. (**Wastes of monopolistic competition**)

38. Consumer interests are not maximized within a monopolistically competitive market setting. The monopolistic firm's product price exceeds MC. In contrast, consumer interests are maximized within purely competitive markets since product price equals MC and minimum AC as well. (**Wastes of monopolistic competition**)

39. Critics of advertising argue that it results in perceived product differentiation, which contributes to increased barriers to entry within the industry. As a result, it is argued that advertising can substantially lessen competition and increase concentration within industrial markets. (**Advertising**)

40. The proponents of advertising argue that it tends to intensify competition within the market. Effective advertising lessens concentration by enhancing consumer awareness of other products and increases vigorous product competition among firms within an industry. (**Advertising**)

Grade Yourself

Circle the numbers of the questions you missed, then fill in the total incorrect for each topic. If you answered more than three questions incorrectly, you need to focus on that topic. (If a topic has less than three questions and you had at least one wrong, we suggest you study that topic also. Read your textbook, or a review book, or ask your teacher for help.)

Subject: The Pure Monopoly and Monopolistically Competitive Market Structures

Topic	Question Numbers	Number Incorrect
Pure monopoly	1, 2, 3, 4, 5, 6, 7, 8	
Price, profits, and costs	9, 10, 11, 12, 13, 14	
Price discrimination	15, 16, 17	
Natural monopoly	18, 19, 20, 21	
Monopolistic competition	22, 23, 24	
Product differentiation	25, 26, 27, 28	
Profits and losses	29, 30, 31, 32	
Wastes of monopolistic competition	33, 34, 35, 36, 37, 38	
Advertising	39, 40	

The Oligopoly Market Structure

8

Brief Yourself

The market structure of oligopoly is characterized by a few large-sized firms that account for a large portion of total industry production and sales. The existence of the "big four" or "big five" typically explains the relative dominance of the select largest firms within an oligopolistic setting, even though there may exist a large number of producers. The products being produced may be standardized and highly substitutable or very differentiated, particularly within consumer goods industries.

The level of market concentration tends to be quite high within oligopolistic industries and is often attributable to prohibitive barriers to entry. Advertising, economies of scale, technological requirements, and legal patent issues are some of the major causes of entry barriers and market concentration within these industries.

Mutual interdependence is a dominant characteristic of oligopolistic industries. It comes from an awareness and recognition among the industry firms that forceful and vigorous price competition would be mutually disadvantageous. Thus, uniformity of price among the industry firms is common, and the firms tend to exercise parallel pricing strategies. This form of proportional price changes to a new uniform level is commonly called price leadership. It is an example of tacit collusion that is permissible under the nation's antitrust laws. In contrast, overt collusion represents a recorded and documented effort among industry firms to manipulate industry market conditions. This form of industry behavior is illegal under the nation's antitrust laws.

Test Yourself

1. What is an oligopolistic industry?

2. Do oligopolies exhibit levels of economic concentration?

3. Are oligopolistic characteristics evident within both consumer goods and capital goods industries?

4. Are the products of oligopolistic producers standardized or differentiated in nature?

5. What are some examples of oligopoly in the production of consumer goods?

6. What is the most prominent form of oligopolistic market behavior?

7. What is mutual interdependence?

8. What is tacit collusion?

9. Is tacit collusion illegal?

10. What is overt collusion?

11. What is an example of illegal overt collusion?

12. What is the kinked oligopolistic demand curve?

13. Explain oligopolistic industry behavior within the range of higher prices.

14. Explain oligopolistic industry behavior within the range of lower prices.

15. What is oligopolistic price leadership behavior?

16. What is barometric price leadership?

17. Is price leadership behavior illegal?

18. What are some measures of economic concentration within the economy?

19. What is a concentration ratio?

20. The four-firm concentration ratio for the breakfast cereal industry is eighty-six percent. What does that mean?

21. What are possible shortcomings of the concentration ratio as a measure of market concentration?

22. What is an Herfindahl Index?

23. What does the gap in the marginal revenue function of the oligopolistic kinked demand curve represent?

24. What happens if oligopolistic firms experience cost increases beyond the range of the gap?

25. Are oligopolistic firms likely to experience both short- and long-run economic profits?

26. What is a cartel?

27. What is an example of an international cartel?

28. Are cartel arrangements permissible under U.S. antitrust laws? Is the OPEC cartel legal?

29. What does the Webb-Pomerene Export Trade Act permit?

30. What is cost-plus pricing?

31. Compared to the purely competitive norm, is productive efficiency optimized under oligopolistic markets?

32. Are consumer interests optimally realized under oligopoly?

33. What arguments are introduced to support oligopolistic industries and technological changes?

34. What other benefits may evolve from these supportive arguments?

35. Does empirical evidence support these claims?

Check Yourself

1. Oligopoly consists of an industrial structure that is dominated by a select few large-sized firms. **(Oligopoly)**

2. Oligopolistic industries tend to be concentrated in nature. There may be a large number of firms within the industry, but a few producers account for the largest share of total industry production and sales. **(Oligopoly)**

3. Oligopoly characterizes both consumer and capital goods industries. Capital goods industries that require high levels of capitalization and consumer good industries that rely upon advertising and trademarked products tend to be oligopolistic in nature. **(Oligopoly)**

4. The products of capital good producers tend to be standardized in nature. The nation's steel industry, aluminum industry, and machine tool producers tend to make standardized products. In contrast, consumer goods producers tend to differentiate their products to reduce the degree of substitutability. This is often the result of high levels of product advertising. **(Oligopoly)**

5. Examples of oligopolistic consumer goods industries include: bicycles, breakfast cereals, canned soups, cigarettes, alcoholic beverages, greeting cards, and soda pop. **(Oligopoly)**

6. The most evident form of oligopolistic behavior is mutual interdependence. **(Mutual interdependence)**

7. Mutual interdependence is an awareness and recognition among the industry firms that uniform selling prices should be maintained. The industry firms seek to avoid competing among each other on the basis of price differences. **(Mutual interdependence)**

8. Tacit collusion is a characteristic of oligopolistic mutual interdependence. Industry firms do not communicate their intent to maintain uniform product prices and avoid competition. Rather, they recognize that vigorous price competition could be ruinous to the industry. **(Mutual interdependence)**

9. Tacit oligopolistic market behavior is not illegal under the nation's antitrust laws. It is legally called the Doctrine of Conscious Parallelism. **(Mutual interdependence)**

10. Overt collusion is illegal under the nation's antitrust laws because the firms purposely seek to communicate their intent to eliminate competition among themselves. **(Mutual interdependence)**

11. It is illegal for two direct competitors within the same market to meet to exchange information, or communicate directly their intent to fix product prices. **(Mutual interdependence)**

12. The kinked demand curve illustrated in Fig. 8.1 (on the following page) is a representation of oligopolistic mutual interdependence. **(Mutual interdependence)**

13. The uniform oligopoly industry price is approximated at the kink in the demand curves at Point P. The industry price is OP_m. For any price above the industry price of OP_m, the demand curve is relatively elastic in nature. This means that no one firm would increase price unless all other industry firms comparably increased their product prices to the new higher industry level. **(Mutual interdependence)**

14. For any price below the industry price of OP_m, the demand curve is relatively inelastic in nature. This suggests that industry firms would seek to avoid vigorous price competition because decreases in prices would result in decreases in their total revenues. **(Mutual interdependence)**

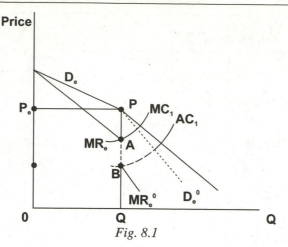

Fig. 8.1

15. Oligopolistic price leadership behavior suggests that one industry firm, typically the largest producer, is the first to initiate the product price change. All other industry firms will then change their product prices to the higher uniform industry norm. **(Price leadership)**

16. Barometric price leadership is a version of price leadership that exists when a smaller and less dominant firm within the oligopoly is the first to initiate the industry price change. It is intended to test any possible adverse market response to the announced price change. Other industry firms will then announce corresponding price changes. **(Price leadership)**

17. Price leadership is not illegal if it represents mutual interdependence and tacit behavior. **(Price leadership)**

18. Measures of economic concentration include concentration ratios and the Herfindahl Index. **(Concentration measures)**

19. A concentration measure is a quantitative measure of the structural characteristics of an industry. The concentration ratio measures the proportion or percent of total industry production or sales attributable to the industry's four, eight, twelve, or more largest companies. **(Concentration measures)**

20. A four-firm concentration ratio is a measure of the proportion or share of total industry output and sales that is attributable to the four largest firms in the industry. A four-firm concentration ratio of eighty-six percent means that the four largest cereal producers account for eighty-six percent of total industry output and market sales. **(Concentration measures)**

21. Concentration measures of industries may vary depending upon the geographical bounds of the markets. A concentration ratio for the national market may not be an accurate measure of more local or regional industry conditions. In addition, concentration ratios as a measure of domestic market conditions may not accurately indicate the impact of foreign trade and import penetration into domestic markets. **(Concentration measures)**

22. As a measure of economic concentration, the Herfindahl Index is the sum of the squared market shares of all firms within the industry. **(Concentration measures)**

23. The marginal revenue gap in the oligopolistic kinked demand curve is illustrated by Points A and B in Fig. 8.1 above. It suggests that the oligopoly industry price will remain constant as long as changes in the firms' marginal costs lie within the range of the marginal revenue gap. **(Marginal revenue gap)**

24. An increase in industry costs that exceeds the upper range of the MR gap beyond Point A will than result in price leadership behavior and a new and higher uniform industry price. (**Marginal revenue gap**)

25. All or most oligopolistic firms tend to incur both short and long-run economic profits in which price exceeds average costs of production. (**Oligopoly and pure competition**)

26. A cartel is an overt collusive organization of competitors within the same industry to manipulate and control their product markets. (**Cartels**)

27. A dominant international cartel is OPEC, the Organization of Petroleum Exporting Countries. Its members consist of the world's major crude oil producers who establish crude oil extraction quotas. This agreement seeks to limit world supply of crude oil and artificially inflate prices. (**Cartels**)

28. Cartel arrangements are illegal under U.S. antitrust laws. This prohibition applies to domestic producers in both the domestic and international markets. The exception to this policy is the exemptive provisions of the Webb-Pomerene Act of 1918. The OPEC cartel is legal because international cartels are not governed by any nation's laws. (**Cartels**)

29. The Webb-Pomerene Act permits U.S. firms within the same industries to form export trade associations that are similar to export cartels. Under these arrangements, the U.S. firms may finalize collusive price fixing, market-sharing, and production agreements for export purposes solely. (**Cartels**)

30. Cost-plus pricing is a method of determining product prices. To establish the price, the firm adds a fixed mark-up on the unit cost of production. This provides the firm with a means of earning a certain rate of profit on its sales. (**Cartels**)

31. Since long-run adjustments and normal profits are not probable for oligopolistic firms, it is likely that average costs are not at their lowest level. Thus, unlike the purely competitive norm, least-cost resource and production efficiency is not attained within oligopolistic market structures. (**Oligopoly and pure competition**)

32. Consumer interests are not optimized within oligopolistic industries. Since long-run economic profits are likely to persist, it is not likely that long-run product prices equal minimum average costs of production within oligopolistic industries. (**Oligopoly and pure competition**)

33. Proponents argue that large oligopolies have the financial resources and human expertise needed to ensure product research and development as well as advances in technology. (**Oligopoly and pure competition**)

34. Oligopoly proponents argue that research and development that leads to new technology and new products will increase standards of living and provide new opportunities for subsequent generations. The more immediate impact of new products and technology may be newly created employment opportunities, new industries, and increased economic prosperity. (**Oligopoly and pure competition**)

35. The empirical research is inconclusive. Many studies confirm that a large portion of industrial research is conducted by relatively large-sized firms. However, other studies suggest that the largest portion of patented new technology and products are the result of research conducted by relatively smaller-sized firms or the independent initiative of a single inventor. (**Oligopoly and pure competition**)

Grade Yourself

Circle the numbers of the questions you missed, then fill in the total incorrect for each topic. If you answered more than three questions incorrectly, you need to focus on that topic. (If a topic has less than three questions and you had at least one wrong, we suggest you study that topic also. Read your textbook, or a review book, or ask your teacher for help.)

Subject: The Oligopoly Market Structure

Topic	Question Numbers	Number Incorrect
Oligopoly	1, 2, 3, 4, 5	
Mutual interdependence	6, 7, 8, 9, 10, 11, 12, 13, 14	
Price leadership	15, 16, 17	
Concentration measures	18, 19, 20, 21, 22	
Marginal revenue gap	23, 24	
Economic profits	25	
Cartels	26, 27, 28, 29, 30	
Oligopoly and pure competition	31, 32, 33, 34, 35	

The Resource Markets

9

Brief Yourself

Resource markets are markets for the resources used in the production of goods and services. Resource markets are traditionally classified into three basic types—those for labor, land, and the funds that can be used for investment or "capital." Much of the supply of these resources, especially labor, comes directly from people rather than firms, the same people who, in product markets, act as consumers. The demand for resources comes not from consumers but from firms that have what is called a "derived demand" for resources. That is, the demand for them is derived from the demand for the products that firms sell to consumers.

The payments to consumers for resources are used by consumers to buy goods and services. Changes in resource prices directly alter discretionary household incomes and immediately influence business sales and profits. Thus, resource pricing is a major determinant of cyclical changes within the economy.

In order to maximize profits, a firm must minimize its production costs. This necessitates the employment of the least-cost combination of resources in production. The prices paid for resources (wages and salaries in the case of labor, interest in the case of capital, rent in the case of land) are important in determining the incomes of the people who own and sell these resources. Of greatest interest are wages and salaries, since these are very large in magnitude for the economy as a whole and are the major source of income for most people. Changes in wages and salaries are of great interest partly because they have an immediate impact on consumer spending and the overall state of the economy.

The demand for a resource is a derived demand because it is dependent upon the final purchase of finished production. Marginal revenue product incorporates the marginal productivity of the resource and the revenue collected by the firm from the sale of the product.

Test Yourself

1. What do the resource markets represent?

2. What are the noted resources and their respective prices?

3. What direct impact do resource prices have upon the economy?

4. How does the pursuit of profit maximization and cost minimization relate to resource prices and employment?

5. What is the nature of a resource-demand function?

6. What is the relationship between changes in resource prices and resource employment?

7. What is marginal revenue product (MRP)?

8. What is marginal resource cost (MRC)?

9. Within competitive resource markets, what is the principle of least-cost resource use?

10. Illustrate purely competitive resource market pricing and employment for the individual firms.

11. What is the similarity between product and resource pricing within a competitive market setting?

12. In addition to prices, what other factors influence derived demand for resources?

13. How will changes in relative resource prices alter the demand for a resource?

14. Can there be a complementary relationship among resources used in production?

15. Summarize some resource non-price changes that would result in an increased resource demand, which would be exhibited as a rightward shift.

16. What is the elasticity of resource demand?

17. What does inelasticity of resource demand mean?

18. What does an elastic resource demand suggest?

19. What would unitary elasticity of resource demand represent?

20. Is the degree of resource substitutability a determinant of resource elasticity of demand?

21. How does the demand elasticity for products affect resource elasticity of demand?

22. Will the proportion of a firm's total costs that are attributable to an employed resource have an impact upon the elasticity of demand for that resource? Explain.

23. What is the least-cost combination of resources to be employed in the production process?

24. What is the difference between nominal and real income?

25. How are wages determined within competitive resource markets?

26. Do individual firms within competitive labor markets dictate wage rate payments?

27. What is a monopsony?

28. Is a monopsonist a wage taker?

29. Illustrate likely wage and employment determination within a monopsonistic market compared to competitive resource conditions.

30. What is the impact upon labor resources under monopsonistic and competitive resource markets?

31. What is bilateral monopoly?

32. What is meant by the phrase "an investment in human capital"?

33. What is economic rent?

34. What is the resource payment for the use of capital and financial resources in production?

35. What is the loanable-funds theory of interest?

36. What does the demand for loanable funds represent?

37. Why is the demand for loanable funds negatively sloped?

38. What determines the supply of loanable funds represent?

39. Why is the supply of loanable funds positively sloped?

40. What is the equilibrium rate of interest in the loanable funds market?

41. What does the equilibrium interest rate mean with respect to investment and savings flows?

42. What contributes to different interest rates paid for different types of investments?

43. What is the pure rate of interest?

44. What allocative function do interest rates assume?

45. What impact do interest rates have upon the economy?

Check Yourself

1. Resource markets represent the interaction of demand and supply for various resources. The demand function represents the potential employment of resources at different prices, while supply exhibits the willingness of resource owners to make their resources available for employment at different prices. **(Resource market)**

2. The noted employable resources and their prices include:

   a. labor-wages, salaries, and commissions paid

   b. land-rental payments

   c. capital-interest, dividend, and capital-gains distributions **(Resource market)**

3. The prices paid to resource owners constitute incomes that are then spent to purchase finished goods and services. Changes in resource prices have a direct impact upon cyclical changes in the economy. **(Resource market)**

4. Firms strive to maximize profits and minimize their costs of production. Resource prices are costs, and businesses seek to employ those quantities and combinations of resources that minimize their production costs. **(Resource market)**

5. A demand function for a resource is a derived demand. This means that the level of resources used depends upon the marginal physical product of the resource employed and the revenue received from the sale of the produced product. **(Derived demand)**

6. The derived demand for a resource is negatively sloped, and the quantity demanded of a resource will vary inversely with changes in resource prices. Prices increase, units demanded decrease, and price decreases increase the level of resource employment. **(Derived demand)**

7. The marginal revenue product (MRP) schedule is the derived demand curve for a resource. It is computed from the marginal physical product (MPP) of the resource and the selling price or marginal revenue derived from the sale of the product. It is the increase in the firm's revenue resulting from the employment of each additional unit of a resource. **(Derived demand)**

8. Marginal resource cost (MRC) is the change in a firm's total resource costs that results from the employment of an additional unit of a variable resource. **(MRP = MRC)**

9. Additional resources should be employed as long as the MRP derived by the firm exceeds the MRC incurred from its use. The MRP = MRC rule states that the optimal and least-cost quantities of employed resources is obtained when the MRP of the last unit employed is equal to its MRC. **(MRP = MRC)**

10. Resource pricing and employment under competitive market conditions is illustrated in Fig. 9.1 on the following page. The competitive market forces of demand and supply determine the market resource price of P_r. The market-determined resource price represents the cost or the MRC to each individual firm within the industry. Given supply or MRC and its demand (MRP), the resource price is OP_r and the firm's level of resource employment is OQ. **(MRP = MRC)**

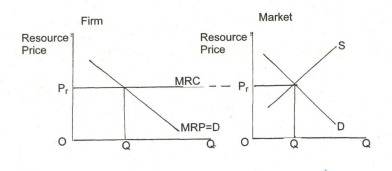

Fig. 9.1

11. The resource market determines resource prices, and the product market determines the prices of finished products and services. Consequently, the representative competitive firm has no control over either the product or the resource price. Both prices are determined by conditions within their respective markets and the firm accepts the price as given. (**MRP = MRC**)

12. Any different process or methodology that changes productivity will alter the MRP for the resource. Innovations, new methods of doing things, and the introduction of technology will impact upon the MPP of a resource and affect its derived demand. This would be exhibited as a shift in the demand function. (**Determinants of demand**)

13. Changes in the price of one consumer product will have an impact upon the consumption of other products. Similarly, changes in the price of a given resource will alter the demand for other resources. Depending upon the degree of resource substitutability, an increase in the cost of capital will likely increase the demand for labor. (**Determinants of demand**)

14. A complementary relationship exists among resources if they are employed and used in a fixed proportion in the production process. If output is to be increased, more of both resources need to be employed. (**Determinants of demand**)

15. The following examples reflect an increase in the derived demand for a resource (exhibited as a rightward shift):

    a. The price of a complementary resource decreases, which would increase the potential employment of all resources and increase production.

    b. The introduction of new technology expands the product market and increases the employment of resources.

    c. New innovations increase the MPP of a given resource.

    d. Retraining and educational programs that increase the MPP of labor would likely increase the demand for that resource. (**Determinants of demand**)

16. Elasticity of resource demand measures the degree of producer responsiveness to changes in resource prices. Like price elasticity of demand for products, the elasticity of resource demand may be elastic or inelastic in nature. (**Resource elasticity**)

17. An inelastic resource demand means that producers are not very responsive to changes in resource prices. Specifically, the percentage change in the amount of the resource employed is less than the percentage change in resource price. (**Resource elasticity**)

18. An elastic resource demand means that producers are very sensitive and responsive to changes in resource prices. The percentage change in the level of resources employed is greater than the percentage change in resource price. (**Resource elasticity**)

19. Unitary elasticity of resource demand would represent proportional changes in the amount of resources employed equal to the proportional change in resource prices. (**Resource elasticity**)

20. The resource demand function will exhibit increased elasticity with greater levels of resource substitution. A lower level of resource substitution suggests a more inelastic resource demand. (**Resource elasticity**)

21. In general, resource demand will be more elastic when the demand for the finished product is also elastic. In contrast, resource elasticity will be more inelastic when the demand for the product is inelastic. (**Resource elasticity**)

22. The resource demand function tends to be more elastic when the employment of a resource constitutes a relatively large proportion of total production costs. In contrast, resource demand tends to be inelastic when resource costs represent a small proportion of total production costs. (**Resource elasticity**)

23. The least-cost combination of resources to be employed at any level of output is approximated when the MPP of a resource with respect to its price is equal to the MPP of all other resources employed with respect to their prices. Thus, least cost is:

$$MPP_L/P_L = MPP_K/P_K, \text{ etc.} \qquad \textbf{(Resource elasticity)}$$

24. Nominal income represents the money payment of wages, etc., received per hour of day or week or whatever period of time. Real income is the actual purchasing power of the money payment that is received. It is a function of the amount of goods and services that can be actually purchased with the money income. (**Wage determination**)

25. Labor-market conditions of demand and supply determine the competitive wage, which is constant for the individual firms within the product markets. (**Wage determination**)

26. It is assumed that each competitive firm employs a relatively small portion of the labor force and therefore does not influence wage determination. Rather, the individual firm accepts the market-determined wage as a given in its employment decisions. (**Wage determination**)

27. Monopsony is defined as a non-competitive type of resource market. It has one dominant producer within the defined resource market who is able to direct and dictate resource-market conditions. (**Monopsony**)

28. A monopsonist is not a wage taker. Monoponists are "wage-makers" because of their dominant presence within their resource markets. (**Monopsony**)

29. Wage and employment determination within competitive and monopsonistic resource markets is illustrated in Fig. 9.2 on the following page. The monopsonist will employ OQ_m of labor as determined at Point A where MRP equals MRC. At that level of employment, the firm will pay a wage of OW_m. In contrast, a competitive firm's resource supply is also its MRC function. Thus, the competitive firm will employ OQ_c amounts of labor as determined at Point C where MRP would approximate MRC. It would pay a wage of OW_c. (**Monopsony**)

30. The level of resource employment would be less under monopsony conditions. In addition, the wage rates would tend to be less than those paid under competitive resource market conditions. (**Monopsony**)

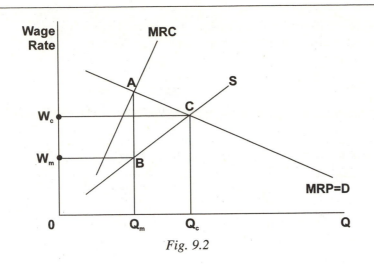

Fig. 9.2

31. Bilateral monopoly implies the presence of a dominant firm on both the demand and supply sides of markets. It suggests a monopolistic producer of finished products interacting with a monopsonistic union as a seller of labor resources. (**Monopsony**)

32. A human capital investment results from expenditures for the education, training, and vocational skill development of individuals within labor markets. Education is like capital equipment in that its purchase is expected to yield benefits, many of them financial, for a number of years into the future. (**Resource payments**)

33. Economic rents are payments for the use of land and other natural resources in the production process. These types of resources are often fixed and exhibit perfect supply inelasticity. (**Resource payments**)

34. Interest rates to a business are the cost of borrowing investment funds. Interest is a resource payment for the use of capital. Other resource payments for the use of capital include capital gain and dividend distributions on purchased debt instruments. (**Resource payments**)

35. The loanable funds theory of interest indicates that demand and supply for capital or loanable funds determines the rate of interest. (**Loanable funds market**)

36. The demand for loanable funds represents the need of businesses to borrow capital for productive investment purposes. The demand for loanable funds is shown in Fig. 9.3 as a negatively sloped function of the interest rate. (**Loanable funds market**)

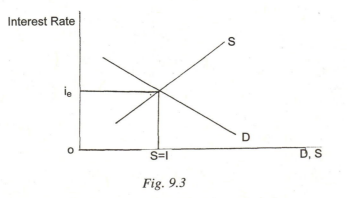

Fig. 9.3

37. The demand for loanable funds responds inversely to changes in the rate of interest (the cost of borrowing). Higher interest rates discourage borrowing, and lower rates encourage borrowing. **(Loanable funds market)**

38. The supply of loanable funds shows the availability of money to be borrowed by businesses for investment purposes. It is a result of savings or non-consumption of income on behalf of consumers. **(Loanable funds market)**

39. The supply of loanable funds responds directly to changes in the rate of interest, which represents the reward or payment for abstinence or savings. Higher interest rates encourage additional savings, and lower rates decrease the reward for non-consumption or savings. **(Loanable funds market)**

40. The equilibrium rate of interest in the loanable funds market is determined by demand and supply. It is the interest rate i_e in Fig. 9.3 where the quantity demanded of loanable funds equals the quantity supplied. **(Loanable funds market)**

41. Investment plans of businesses are equal to the savings plans of consumers at the equilibrium rate of interest. **(Loanable funds market)**

42. Differences in interest rates reflect varied levels of risk in the investment, differences in the length or maturity of a loan, the size of the loan, and the various tax implications of a loan. **(Interest rates)**

43. The pure rate of interest is the interest paid for an investment in relatively long-term, riskless debt instruments of the national government. **(Investment rates)**

44. Interest rates allocate capital or financial funds into different productive ventures that are anticipated to be profitable in response to producer demands. **(Interest rates)**

45. Interest rates influence and direct business investment and consumer spending, which determine aggregate expenditures on goods and services. This influences cyclical changes within the economy. **(Interest rates)**

Grade Yourself

Circle the numbers of the questions you missed, then fill in the total incorrect for each topic. If you answered more than three questions incorrectly, you need to focus on that topic. (If a topic has less than three questions and you had at least one wrong, we suggest you study that topic also. Read your textbook, or a review book, or ask your teacher for help.)

Subject: The Resource Markets

Topic	Question Numbers	Number Incorrect
Resource market	1, 2, 3, 4	
Derived demand	5, 6, 7	
MRP = MRC	8, 9, 10, 11	
Determinants of demand	12, 13, 14, 15	
Resource elasticity	16, 17, 18, 19, 20, 21, 22, 23	
Wage determination	24, 25, 26	
Monopsony	27, 28, 29, 30, 31	
Resource payments	32, 33, 34	
Loanable funds market	35, 36, 37, 38, 39, 40, 41	
Interest rates	42, 43, 44, 45	

Contemporary Economic Issues

10

Brief Yourself

The purpose of economic analysis is to identify and resolve both domestic and international issues. Critical to most, if not all, of these issues is the appropriate role of government. Should the laissez-faire philosophy be preserved and emphasis exclusively placed upon the ability of the market mechanism to respond optimally to the allocative and distributive needs of the society? Or should a more active government role be advanced to correctly resolve the pressing economic needs that exist?

The public debt and the issue of deficit spending influences the immediate and long-term policy alternatives for the nation. While substantial advances have been made in the economic well-being of most Americans over the past several generations, an alarmingly large number of individuals and families continue to experience poverty and a bleak future.

The U.S. has enjoyed an agricultural revolution. A relatively small portion of the nation's population produces an excess abundance, which jeopardizes both the incomes and long-run prosperity of farm families. Similarly, the presence of industrial concentration within domestic markets jeopardizes the functional effectiveness of the market system. Monopolistic elements impact upon the well-being of consumers and the long-run direction of the nation's economy.

The competitive position of domestic firms within international markets has significantly eroded. This is evident from the deficit in the nation's balance-of-payments and its net international debt position.

Test Yourself

1. What is industrial or market concentration?

2. What arguments are commonly used against industrial concentration?

3. What arguments are often introduced in support of industrial concentration?

4. What are antitrust laws?

5. What is the jurisdictional application of the nation's antitrust laws?

6. What is interstate commerce?

7. What is intrastate commerce?

8. What are the primary prohibitions contained in the Sherman Act of 1890?

9. What types of business behavior constitute restraint of trade?

10. What are treble damages?

11. What are the noted provisions of the Clayton Act of 1914?

12. When is price discrimination or selling to different customers at different prices permissible under the Clayton Act?

13. What are tying contracts?

14. What are the functions of the Federal Trade Commission?

15. What is the Wheeler-Lea Act?

16. What is the Celler-Kefauver Act of 1950?

17. Explain the interpretative implications of the Rule of Reason Doctrine.

18. What is the Reversed Rule of Reason Doctrine?

19. Did the Alcoa Case of 1945 rest upon the Reversed Rule of Reason Doctrine?

20. What is a horizontal merger?

21. What is a vertical merger?

22. What is a conglomerate merger?

23. Is the demand for agricultural products elastic or inelastic?

24. What are the implications of inelastic demand upon farm prices and incomes?

25. What have been the more important long run characteristics of the American agricultural industry?

26. What is the purpose of farm price supports that are maintained by the government?

27. What has been the long-run impact of price supports upon agricultural production?

28. What is an important provision of the Farm Act of 1990?

29. What is a Lorenz curve?

30. What are some of the major factors that contribute to income inequalities within the population?

31. Has the measured incidence of poverty increased or decreased within the nation in recent years?

32. What is a nation's balance of trade?

33. What is the current account of a nation's balance of payments?

34. What are credit and debit transactions in a nation's balance of trade?

35. What is the capital account of a nation's balance of payments?

36. What are a nation's so-called Official Reserves?

37. How are exchange rates determined?

38. What conditions influence market-exchange-rate conditions?

39. What is exchange-rate depreciation?

40. What is exchange-rate appreciation?

41. What is the impact of exchange-rate depreciation upon a nation's exports and imports?

42. What is the impact of exchange-rate appreciation upon a nation's exports and imports?

43. What is the Gold Standard?

44. What is direct investment?

45. How is the U.S. balance-of-payments deficit related to the nation's foreign indebtedness?

46. What is a tariff?

47. Explain two different types of tariffs.

48. Illustrate the effects of a no-tariff policy.

49. What is the impact of an imposed tariff upon imports?

50. What is the amount of revenue received by government from the imposition of the tariff?

✓ Check Yourself

1. Industrial concentration relates to the level of monopoly power within product markets. It exists when a few large firms account for a relatively large amount of industry production and sales. (**Industrial concentration**)

2. Critics of industrial concentration argue that monopoly power jeopardizes the market system and the well-being of consumers through high prices and misallocation of resources. It is additionally suggested that market power can have a direct impact upon the political environment within a nation. (**Industrial concentration**)

3. Supporters of industrial concentration argue that non–price competition is vigorous among larger-sized firms. In addition, the larger firms have the resources to conduct risky research and development that leads to new products and technological advances. (**Industrial concentration**)

4. Congress has enacted antitrust laws as a means of promoting and preserving competitive market conditions. They prohibit certain predatory forms of firm behavior and additionally decree that uncontrolled monopoly is illegal. (**Antitrust laws**)

5. The nation's antitrust laws apply to domestic businesses engaged in domestic interstate and international commerce. They equally apply to foreign businesses that engage in commerce within the U.S. (**Antitrust laws**)

6. Interstate commerce is business activity that is conducted among states. The nation's federal antitrust laws apply to interstate commerce. (**Antitrust laws**)

7. Intrastate commerce is business activity that is contained within an individual state. The federal antitrust laws do not apply to intrastate commerce. (**Antitrust laws**)

8. The Sherman Act forbids efforts to monopolize or to create a monopoly in interstate and international commerce. It additionally decrees that restraint of trade is illegal. (**Antitrust laws**)

9. Illegal restraint of trade activities include collusive agreements among industry firms to fix selling prices, establish market sharing agreements, or impose production or sales quotas within different markets. (**Antitrust laws**)

10. Treble damages are a form of financial restitution made to injured parties. That restitution is three times the level of estimated damages. (**Antitrust laws**)

11. The noted prohibitions of the Clayton Act declare that price discrimination is illegal, that reciprocity and tying contracts are illegal, that interlocking directorates may be illegal, and that stock acquisition mergers may be illegal if they result in excess monopoly power. (**Antitrust laws**)

12. Businesses may charge different customers different prices when the quantities purchased are different, the quality of the products is different, and the sales are in different markets that result in differences in transportation costs. (**Antitrust laws**)

13. Tying contracts represent an illegal effort to obligate a buyer to purchase other unneeded products or services as a condition of sale. **(Antitrust laws)**

14. The law established the FTC as a government regulatory agency to investigate competitive conditions within industries. The FTC can litigate business practices it considers to be unfair and illegal. **(Antitrust laws)**

15. The Wheeler-Lea Act of 1938 granted the FTC the power to evaluate and prosecute misleading and fraudulent advertising. **(Antitrust laws)**

16. The Celler-Kefauver Act was enacted to strengthen the anti-merger Section Seven provision of the Clayton Act. It decrees that mergers consummated through asset purchases that result in excess monopoly power are illegal. **(Antitrust laws)**

17. The Rule of Reason Doctrine is a judicial interpretation of monopoly that places emphasis upon the behavior and performance of the firm or firms. Monopoly structures within an industry are not illegal if there is no evidence of anti-competitive and abusive behavior. Thus, a good monopoly is permissible, only a bad monopoly is to be condemned. **(Judicial interpretation)**

18. The Reversed Rule of Reason Doctrine is an alternate interpretation of monopoly that places emphasis upon the structural characteristics of the firm and industry. Any monopoly, whether good or bad, is illegal. **(Judicial interpretation)**

19. The Alcoa Company has always maintained an excessive and dominant presence with a market share of over ninety percent. During litigation, the company argued that it never abused its monopoly power and indeed successfully advanced the interests of consumers and the nation. Nevertheless, the court decreed that all monopolies, not just bad monopolies, are illegal, thus resting on the Reversed Rule of Reason Doctrine. **(Judicial interpretation)**

20. A horizontal merger is an acquisition among firms that were formerly direct rivals and competitors. A merger between Ford and GM would be an example of a horizontal merger. **(Mergers)**

21. A vertical merger is an acquisition of firms that were formerly in a supplier and manufacturer relationship. A merger between the Du Pont and GM companies would be an example of a vertical merger. **(Mergers)**

22. A conglomerate merger represents an acquisition among firms that are producing unrelated products. **(Mergers)**

23. The aggregate demand for agricultural products tends to be very inelastic. Within specific food-product groups, however, there may exist degrees of product substitutability. **(Food-price elasticity)**

24. The inelastic demand means that small increases in harvest will result in disproportionately larger decreases in food prices for agricultural products, which will reduce the incomes of farm families. **(Food-price elasticity)**

25. Advances in agricultural technology have resulted in substantial increases in productivity and output. In contrast, the consumption of agricultural products has increased at slow rates over the same period of time. With inelastic price and income demands, these conditions would lead to significantly lower market prices and farm incomes. **(Food-price elasticity)**

26. Farm price supports are established by the government to ensure that farmers will receive minimum prices for their production. **(Agricultural programs)**

27. Price supports have encouraged artificially high levels of production, which have resulted in excess surpluses that have been purchased and maintained by the government. (**Agricultural programs**)

28. In general, the Farm Act of 1990 attempts to reduce farm subsidies paid by government and to encourage farmers to respond to market forces in making production decisions. Specifically, the legislation reduces by fifteen percent the acreage covered by price supports and allows farmers to select crop production in response to market conditions. (**Agricultural programs**)

29. A Lorenz curve graphically summarizes the actual distribution of income among a nation's population. When compared to an ideal or equal income distribution, it shows the incidence of economic inequalities within the population. (**Income inequality**)

30. Some of the more evident determinants of income inequalities include:

    a. differences in the innate abilities of individuals to learn and achieve

    b. differences in vocational training and educational achievement

    c. the socio-economic environment within which a person is born and raised

    d. differences in family wealth that influence the developmental direction and career opportunities of individuals (**Income inequality**)

31. The portion of the nation's total population living in poverty is approximately 13.5 to 14 percent, and it has been increasing during the past decade. (**Income inequality**)

32. A nation's balance of payments tracks international commodity, service, and financial transactions among nations. (**Balance of payments**)

33. The current account relates to international transactions in merchandise wares and services. The current account is negative if imports of goods and services exceed exports. (**Balance of payments**)

34. An export is a credit transaction since it results in an inflow of foreign monies into the nation. An import is a debit transaction since it results in an outflow of money abroad. (**Balance of payments**)

35. The capital account reflects financial flows among nations in the form of purchases or sales of financial assets. The purchases or sale of foreign-issued debt instruments is commonly called Portfolio Investment. (**Balance of payments**)

36. Official reserves are quantities of foreign currency held by a nation's central bank to meet obligations to other nations. (**Balance of payments**)

37. An exchange rate is the price of one currency expressed in terms of another, such as the value of the dollar relative to the pound or yen or franc. Presently, exchange rates are determined by demand and supply conditions within competitive exchange-rate markets. (**Exchange rates**)

38. Demand and supply conditions within the exchange-rate markets will respond to many different conditions, including:

    a. changes in income among nations, which influence export and import trade

    b. changes in product prices among nations, which alters import and export trade

    c. changes in tastes and preferences among consumers, which determines import and export trade among nations

    d. changes in economic conditions, such as interest rates, the money supply, inflation, and budget deficits, within and among nations that may change import and export trade (**Exchanges rates**)

39. Exchange-rate depreciation means that the convertible value of the depreciated currency has decreased in exchange for other currencies. When the dollar depreciates, its value is worth less relative to all other currencies. (**Exchange rates**)

40. Exchange-rate appreciation is an increased convertible value of the appreciated currency in terms of other currencies. When the dollar appreciates, its value is worth more relative to all other currencies. (**Exchange rates**)

41. A depreciated currency would tend to increase the nation's exports and decrease its imports from the rest of the world. (**Exchange rates**)

42. An appreciated currency would tend to decrease the nation's exports and increase its imports. (**Exchange rates**)

43. The Gold Standard establishes fixed exchange rates by requiring nations to peg the value of their domestic currency to gold. (**Exchange rates**)

44. Direct investment represents foreign ownership in the purchase of assets or stock of a domestic business. Foreign direct investment in America would be a foreign business that builds a production or distribution facility in the U.S. (**Trade policy**)

45. The trade deficit in the U.S. balance of payments is financed by the nation's added indebtedness to foreign interests. The U.S. has borrowed increasingly more than it has earned from the rest of the world to pay for the trade deficit, increasing its net debtor status. (**Trade policy**)

46. A tariff is a tax that is imposed upon products imported into a nation. It is intended to increase the selling price of the imported good and discourage consumption. (**Trade policy**)

47. An ad valorem tariff is a percent of the market value of the imported product. A ten percent tariff levy on a one hundred dollar imported product would result in a tariff charge of ten dollars.

    A specific tariff is a fixed dollar amount on each unit of the imported product, regardless of its selling price. A one hundred dollar specific tariff is the same whether it is imposed on an expensive or cheap version of the imported product. (**Trade policy**)

48. The impact of both non-tariff and tariff policies is illustrated in Fig. 10.1. The selling price of the import before the tariff is OP_n. At that low price, domestic quantity demanded (OQ_3) exceeds domestic quantity supplied (OQ), which results in a level of imports of Q_3-Q. (**Trade policy**)

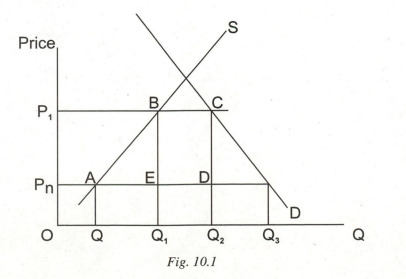

Fig. 10.1

49. Total domestic consumption was reduced to OQ_2 from OQ_3, and domestic production increased from OQ to OQ_1. As a result, the new level of imports was reduced to Q_1 to Q_2 from Q to Q_3. (**Trade policy**)

50. Total tariff revenue received is the total level of imports times the unit value of tariff, which is measured as the increase in price from OP_f to OP_t. Thus, total tariff revenues collected are the rectangular area BCDE. (**Trade policy**)

Grade Yourself

Circle the numbers of the questions you missed, then fill in the total incorrect for each topic. If you answered more than three questions incorrectly, you need to focus on that topic. (If a topic has less than three questions and you had at least one wrong, we suggest you study that topic also. Read your textbook, or a review book, or ask your teacher for help.)

Subject: Contemporary Economic Issues

Topic	Question Numbers	Number Incorrect
Industrial concentration	1, 2, 3	
Antitrust laws	4, 5, 6, 7, 8, 9, 10, 11, 12, 13, 14, 15, 16	
Judicial interpretation	17, 18, 19	
Mergers	20, 21, 22	
Food-price elasticity	23, 24, 25	
Agricultural programs	26, 27, 28	
Income inequality	29, 30, 31	
Balance of payments	32, 33, 34, 35, 36	
Exchange rates	37, 38, 39, 40, 41, 42, 43	
Trade policy	44, 45, 46, 47, 48, 49, 50	

Also Available

. . . and many others to come!